THE ART OF COARSE CRICKET

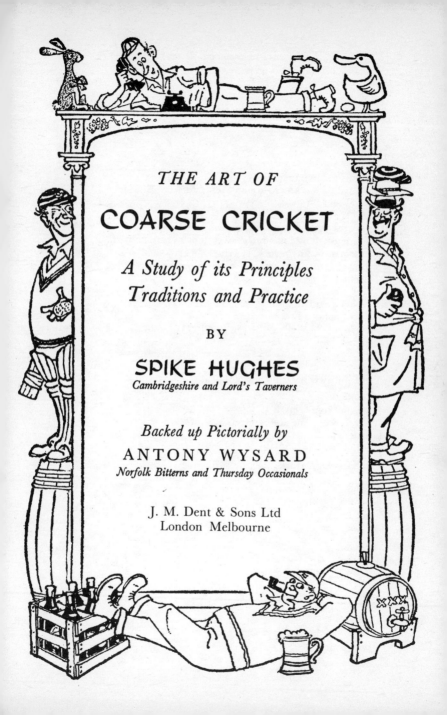

THE ART OF
COARSE CRICKET

*A Study of its Principles
Traditions and Practice*

BY

SPIKE HUGHES
Cambridgeshire and Lord's Taverners

Backed up Pictorially by
ANTONY WYSARD
Norfolk Bitterns and Thursday Occasionals

J. M. Dent & Sons Ltd
London Melbourne

First published in paperback 1986
First published 1954 by Museum Press Ltd

Printed in Great Britain by Guernsey Press Co. Ltd, Guernsey C.I., for
J. M. Dent & Sons Ltd
Aldine House, 33 Welbeck Street, London W1M 8LX

British Library Cataloguing in Publication Data

Hughes, Spike
    The art of coarse cricket.
    1. Cricket——Anecdotes, facetiae, satire, etc.
    I. Title
    796.35′0207   GV919

    ISBN 0-460-02441-8

To the immortal memory of

ARCHIE MACDONNEL

*who, being a Scotsman, inclined to cautious
understatement in his classic study of Coarse
Cricket in 'England, Their England,'
this book is affectionately
dedicated*

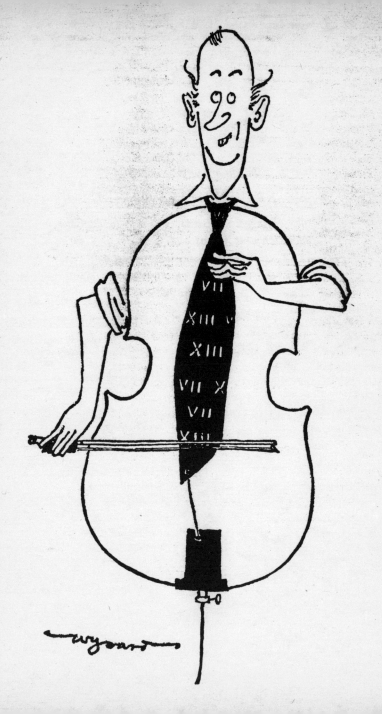

CONTENTS

FOREWORD

BY DENIS COMPTON

Middlesex and England

'COARSE CRICKET!' What a wonderful description of a game we all know so well – whether on the village green, the corners of a public park, or the frequently-interrupted but otherwise timeless 'tests' played with a tennis ball in the school playground. At home, overseas, anywhere on earth where cricket is played for pure enjoyment, there you will find Coarse Cricket. As Spike Hughes rightly suggests, we are all Coarse Cricketers at heart, for whatever our eventual status as players we all began originally by playing Coarse Cricket, and the player is a happy man who can still recapture something of that first carefree spirit in later life.

In his book, Spike has succeeded in recapturing just that spirit. It is not concerned with the actions and achievements of the comparatively few, and it is not written by a mere spectator for other spectators. Results, statistics, averages and the rest have no place in it, for he writes of the way he enjoys his own cricket – which is the way it is enjoyed by thousands of enthusiastic exponents of varying skill, indefatigable spirit and unshakable optimism, for whom, surely, the English summer was specially created.

This is cricket at its gayest; and so long as cricket can be played that way we need have no fear for the future of our great national game.

Denis Compton

If the wild bowler thinks he bowls,
   Or if the batsman thinks he's bowled,
They know not, poor misguided souls,
   They too shall perish unconsoled.
I am the batsman and the bat,
   I am the bowler and the ball,
The umpire, the pavilion cat,
   The roller, pitch, and stumps, and all.

ANDREW LANG
in imitation of Emerson

1. First Principles

COARSE CRICKET, which is often seen but seldom believed, is like coarse fishing: a pastime intended primarily for the almost exclusive unskilled enjoyment of those who practise it. It is a sport more remarkable for the enthusiasm than for the aptitude of its players and is best played against breweries.

The history of Coarse Cricket is the history of cricket

itself. Tell me the name of the first man to swing a cricket bat and I will tell you the name of the original Coarse Cricketer; for there has been no player of cricket, dead or alive, famous or obscure, who did not originally begin by playing Coarse Cricket. W. G. Grace in his Gloucestershire orchard, Bradman with his stump and golf ball, Jack Hobbs on Parker's Piece, Denis Compton bowling his 'Chinaman' with a tennis ball against a lamp-post –

they were all players of Coarse Cricket. The only difference is that whereas they tended to develop and better themselves, the rest of us have remained virtually as we were in the beginning and ever shall be.

If the first principle of Coarse Cricket is that it is a game for the enjoyment of the player, the second principle is undoubtedly that the result of any game played is of the utmost unimportance. It is the Game and How it is Played

which counts, and unless this maxim is recognized by all concerned there can be no such thing as enjoyment by the players, and therefore no such thing as true Coarse Cricket. You might just as well play in a Test Match.

In the ordinary way there may be said to be seven grades of cricket:

> *First-class cricket*
>
> *Minor Counties cricket*
>
> *Club cricket*
>
> *Country-House cricket*
>
> *College and Hospital Cricket* (*non-competitive*)
>
> *School cricket*
>
> *Village cricket*

Coarse Cricket cannot be conveniently ranked among these categories, for Coarse Cricketers can, and often do, find themselves playing in the company of cricketers in each of the above grades. With one exception: no true Coarse Cricketer will ever have anything to do with Club Cricket if he can possibly avoid it.

It is not that some of us are not good enough to play Club Cricket. We are; indeed, I have played several games of characteristically enjoyable, unadulterated Coarse Cricket in the company of a player who has appeared in eight Test Matches for England and took to our code like a duck (which, incidentally, is his highest score to date) to water. It is just that Coarse Cricket and Club Cricket are as irreconcilable as good and evil. They have nothing in common. They differ so vastly in mentality, temperament and surroundings, in their whole social, psychological, technical and ethical approach to the game that you may look in vain for the player of the one sort of cricket in the ranks of those who play the other. Which is as it should be, for Coarse and Club Cricket are chemically incompatible and any attempt to fuse the two elements results only in a malignant and incurable irritation.

No, the neatly trimmed sports ground, with its deck chairs for the ladies placed in front of the brick-built pavilion where the bar doesn't open until 6 o'clock – that is not the soil in which Coarse Cricket can flourish. Coarse Cricket can breathe freely only in the English countryside. It is the cricket of Pub and Ground – and if the Pub owns the Ground, then so much the better.

No Coarse Cricket side, of course, has a home ground of its own. It doesn't need one, for wherever it plays automatically becomes Home. The spirit of true Coarse Cricket is infectious and there are very few occasions when a Coarse team fails to infect (some might say demoralize) opponents who show any reluctance to play cricket *our* way. If, by some mischance, we *should* fail then the remedy is simple: the fixture is not repeated. But that is a mercifully rare occurrence.

You will note that I refer to a Coarse Cricket 'team' and not to a Coarse Cricket 'Eleven'. This is because, as I will show in a later chapter, the organization of an exact XI is not only so difficult as to be almost impossible, but it is also contrary to the long traditions of the game.

Although, as we shall see, the traditions and conventions of Coarse Cricket are strict and unique, it must not be thought that the game itself is played according to any other rules than the latest Laws of Cricket as laid down by M.C.C. Being a free and highly independent people, however, our interpretation of these Laws may vary according to circumstances; but on the whole the rudimentary principles of cricket are adhered to.

The game of Coarse Cricket, on the other hand, must never be regarded as anything but a means to an end. To win a match is a satisfying and exhilarating feeling – or is said to be by those happy few Coarse teams of my acquaintance who have ever won a match – but the first and last object of playing Coarse Cricket at all is to spend a day and an evening in good company and congenial surroundings. For this reason the most frequent scene of Coarse Cricket is the English village; but here again discrimination is sometimes needed and a carelessly arranged fixture against a village team may result in a wasted afternoon against opponents desperately keen to preserve an unbroken record and whose wicket-keeper will grumble loudly about the effect on his average of a leg-bye signalled as a bye.

A good Coarse Cricket match is like the Eton and Harrow match; the only difference being that it is the players who create and enjoy the social side of the affair, not the spectators.

The English village green, then, is the natural Home ground of all Coarse Cricketers wherever they may come from. And they come from all over the place, from all walks of life, and very often, when numerical adjustment has to be made to ensure that the batting order is not a complete blank in the score book after No. 7, from the opponents' village as well.

Not all Coarse Cricket matches, of course, are played only against villages or on village greens. Coarse Cricket can insinuate itself into quite unexpected surroundings, some of them looking suspiciously like Sports Grounds. But when two Coarse teams are playing each other the acrid smell of Club Cricket which may have been left behind by the principal, but fortunately absent, tenants of the ground is dispelled immediately, and the bar is open, or the contents of a bar made available from the moment of the players' arrival until the moment of their departure, which usually coincides with local opening time.

Thus it would be unfair of me to suggest that a rewarding day cannot be spent on the vast and impressively tidy arenas of Guy's Hospital at Honor Oak Park or St George's Hospital at Wimbledon. I have spent pleasant, well-victualled days in both places – deck chairs, brick pavilion and all. Which suggests that, in the end, Coarse Cricket, while at its best in the countryside, can survive transplantation to foreign soil and is largely dependent for its existence on an attitude of mind.

This attitude of mind is fortunately far more common in England than the casual student of cricket might think. I have found it in Oxford and Cambridge colleges, at R.A.F. stations in wartime, in the B.B.C. (though not, naturally, in the B.B.C. team whose exploits against Eton Ramblers and the like are recorded in the Sunday papers. That's all *très* Club); I have found it, too, in the variety profession, on the legitimate stage, among dance band musicians, in film studios, the Territorial Army, the editorial staffs of newspapers, in the London Philharmonic Orchestra, on the private ground of a palatial Worcestershire country house. I have even found it among the publicity men of Wardour Street, whose life, though it may not appear very real to the rest of us, is nevertheless earnest and anything but an empty dream to their mournful numbers.

From these and many other professions, ranks and occupations, then, come the players of Coarse Cricket: the cradle of the great, the nursery of good fellowship and the grave of all who think they already know everything about cricket.

2. Organization

GETTING A FIXTURE. Once you have decided to play Coarse Cricket only the very first fixture will prove at all difficult to come by. Although obviously no hard and fast rules can be laid down about arranging fixtures, it will be found from experience that the average Coarse

Cricket match is the result of knowing somebody whose local village would welcome a visit from a team of Gentlemen from London. Before accepting any challenge, however, it is essential to know something of the amenities and surroundings of the proposed venue. It should not be more than 40 miles from London, as one of the important aspects of any Coarse Cricket fixture is the ability of the Coarse team to be at least twenty-five miles out of London by the time the public houses are open on a Sunday morning. The experienced captain-secretary-treasurer (hereinafter called The Organizer) of any Coarse Cricket side will quickly learn to nominate a particular public house *en route* as the first point of assembly of the day. This, apart from the obvious need for refreshment at mid-day, often enables the Organizer to get some idea of the number of starters he may expect for the match. According to circumstances the number of arrivals at this first stopping place may or may not strike the Organizer with panic and anxiety; but either way the Sunday mid-day halt gives some indication of the Glorious Uncertainty to be expected.

Coarse fixtures, it will be found, tend to beget Coarse fixtures once the initial game has been arranged. A pleasing and successful fixture in May not only often leads to a return visit or two later in the season, but the Organizer will frequently find that among the members of his team is at least one player who knows somebody who knows somebody else who lives in a village. Sometimes fixtures are created even more haphazardly. For several seasons a rubber of three matches was regularly played by my own team against a village on the Great West Road between Maidenhead and Reading, a fixture which began simply because our umpire was a racing man and he knew the owner and trainer of a racing stables opposite the cricket ground.

In arranging a Coarse Cricket match considerable thought must be given to the question of amenities. Geographical considerations are usually against an all-day match; it makes a long day of it all and the earlier part of the morning is spent in an unnecessary scramble across the countryside in order to start play before opening time – a practice which all true Coarse Cricketers regard as uncivilized, involving as it does the loss of at least an hour and a half's valuable drinking time.

It is this question of time and opportunity for drinking which led me to warn all Organizers to think before they accept a challenge from unfamiliar quarters. Is there a pub visible from the ground? If tea is served there during the match, is beer available for those players who do not drink tea? If not, is there going to be beer in barrel or jug in the pavilion? If not, can it be arranged that there is – at the visiting side's expense, if need be?

If the answer to all these questions is 'yes' (and there are happily very few Coarse fixtures I have ever made where the answer is not 'yes'), then you have a fixture which may be considered normal and worth repeating. Ironically the only games I have ever played where the answer to the questions was always 'no' were against a country brewery; but the surroundings were so attractive and the cricket itself so enjoyable that one almost forgot that one was spending an entirely teetotal afternoon. Almost . . .

A fixture card is, of course, entirely superfluous. Even if one's opponents did not send you their list of fixtures for the season, there is not the slightest chance of any Coarse Cricket Organizer forgetting when the next match is to be played, nor of his regular players forgetting either. For, from about the first week in February, when the Organizer begins the season's organizing, he never stops organizing until the leaves are falling in the last week in September.

GETTING A TEAM TOGETHER. Before anything else is considered the Organizer must be provided with a telephone, unlimited patience and perseverance, and almost unlimited money with which to pay the telephone bill when it comes in, for he will find that the cost of telephone calls during the summer months is anything up to seven or eight times more than at any other time of the year. It is not only that the Organizer will have to make an abnormal number of local calls in his efforts to collect a side, but any Coarse Cricket Match entails numberless toll and trunk calls to the place where the game is to be played. These out-of-town calls are the result of the inevitable last-minute S.O.S. appeals to one's opponents to supplement one's team by anything from two to six local players on arrival, and also of frequent and contradictory estimates discussed with the local pub of the number of players, wives and children expected to want luncheon before the match.

In passing, it would be as well to advise the inexperienced Organizer to select, as far as possible, local pubs where sandwiches are available. The sit-down luncheon is a nice idea – for the consumers. For the Organizer it can mean a great many unnecessary extra troubles, not the least of which is the almost impossible task of getting the assembled company to sit down at all even after the landlord's final, desperate appeal to begin eating a meal which has been ready and spoiling for nearly three-quarters of an hour. This reluctance on the part of the majority of Coarse Cricketers to leave the cosy social atmosphere of the bar is unfortunate but understandable; to have to move to another room and sit down at a table interrupts the continuity of social intercourse, and is an obvious argument in favour of the sandwich which can be munched unhurriedly

while the muncher continues to enjoy general group-conversation in the room he has been in for the past couple of hours or so.

Another thing against the sit-down luncheon is that to the Organizer it tends to be an extravagance which leaves him heavily out-of-pocket at the end of the day; for when it comes to collecting the money he will invariably find that many of those who were present at luncheon and whose children, in addition, ate more than three times their share of cakes at teatime, have slipped away early without paying. It is fun to behave as though you were an even richer Sir Julian Cahn (which, let me assure you, Organizers are always having to do and are generally considered to be), but somehow bank managers do not care much for the idea in the end.

These parenthetic observations, however, are of no immediate importance. Coarse Cricket is full of many occupational hazards and the matter of being regularly out-of-pocket at weekends is something the Organizer soon learns to regard as the most trivial of them. The main point of having sandwiches for lunch is that, with any luck, you may be able to persuade the assembled visiting company to accept a form of P.A.Y.E. – Pay As You Eat. This will save many beautiful friendships from foundering on the rocks of sordid and acrimonious financial discussion later in the evening.

While all this goes a long way to solving the problem of pre-match feeding it is by no means the perfect solution. The ideal to aim at is the sort of fixture where the local Organizer (who may be the president or captain of the village side) invites the entire visiting team and its hangers-on to an al fresco fork-luncheon in his garden. Fixtures like this have unfortunately become rare since 1939, but hang on to them with all your might if you can find them and give them all priority among the season's engagements. The local Organizer may expect to be rewarded only in Heaven for his benevolence and hospitality, but in fact he is nearly always rewarded by a grilling hot day for his feast. Indeed, in my experience I have never known one of these occasions to be graced with anything but exceptionally clement summer weather.

Perhaps before reverting to the question of Getting a Team Together it might be advisable to warn the would-be Organizer that Coarse Cricket is a hard taskmaster, that to be a successful Organizer demands the possession of virtues and qualities of character not often encountered among ordinary mortals.

The purely technical side of captaincy will be dealt with in a later chapter; the secretarial work involved in fixture-making and the problems and anxieties facing the office of treasurer have already been hinted at. But in addition to combining these three offices in one person, the Organizer must be several other things besides.

Above all things, he must not be a teetotaller; but perhaps that is a superfluous remark. Coarse Cricket is not an excuse for an alcoholic orgy, but it must be remembered that cricket has always been associated since its earliest days with premises able to quench an Englishman's summer thirst. If cricket was not actually invented at the Bat and Ball at Hambledon, it was a close thing; and the natural association of bat and ball with beer has so long been an unwritten law of the game that, apart from the numberless inns up and down the country called the Cricketers or the Cricketers' Arms, it is an unshakable tradition that the bars of county grounds should be open for half an hour before the advertised time of the beginning of play until half an hour after its close.

Next, the Organizer must have something in him of the schoolteacher – the schoolteacher's patience and authority, his ability to shepherd an undisciplined collection of highly individualistic, un-sheeplike bodies out of the pub on to the ground, off the ground into the dressing-room, out of their clothes into their flannels, out of the dressing-room on to the field. This last operation is no more difficult than the others, but it happens more often – at the start of the match, at the beginning of the second innings and after the tea interval.

Tact and imperturbable diplomacy are also essential virtues, for without them the Organizer will be powerless to disarm often justified criticism that his team is a *little* late, that it is a *little* short of players, and that at least half a dozen of them got a *little* amorous after the game last time and would they please not molest the landlord's daughter of The Cricketers so much this time as she is now a respectable married woman. Useful phrases to deal with these situations will be put forward in the general section on Captaincy.

And finally the Organizer must have a genius for Administration, for without it all is lost; or worse – it is never begun. Whoever is inspired to organize and eventually – if he lives that long – to enjoy a day of Coarse Cricket must

realize one thing from the very beginning: that the invasion of Normandy was a mere off-the-cuff improvisation compared with the planning and co-ordination needed to get eleven players to the same place, on the same day at the same time, without financial inducement, hope of expenses being paid, or the guarantee that a doubtful weather forecast will permit any cricket at all.

The first step in the process of Getting a Team Together is to write down a list of *at least seventeen* possible players. Not, dear Organizer, because you are going to tour Australia for four months; you are not A Selector. You are A Collector, and experience will soon teach you that to have a mere eleven Absolutely Certain and Definite Acceptors on the Wednesday morning is no guarantee whatever of finding yourself with a full eleven on the Sunday morning. Long before the Saturday night that once-so-reassuring and reliable eleven will have dwindled to half its number or less. The reasons for this are many and varied and, as experience will quickly show, none of them is avoidable. It must be said that the defaulters, being true Coarse Cricketers, nearly always inform you of their inability to play, though not always in time to enable you to make alternative arrangements in any comfort. Cases of entirely unheralded absence on the day of the match are happily fairly rare.

To avoid disappointment, however, aim always to field seventeen players, excluding travelling reserves. For in that way you have an even chance of arriving with seven players (in which case you borrow four from the village). or with thirteen (in which case you lend the village one of your players and the game is played 12-a-side). Once in a lifetime I have arrived with fourteen players. It was a

match, on a neutral Buckinghamshire ground borrowed
for the occasion, against the London Irish Rifles, who also
arrived with a full XIV. Only a small proportion of each
side had an innings, for with fourteen fielders the rate of
scoring was inevitably slowed down. The London Irish
batted first and declared at teatime, with only a handful
of wickets down; while for our part no more than four
ineffectual wickets fell by 6.55 p.m., when, according to
the unwritten laws of Coarse Cricket, stumps were
inexorably drawn to enable players and public to be at the
Nag's Head at opening time.

This sort of thing, of course, is exceptional. For the most
part your efforts at Getting a Team Together will be
thwarted by events which you realize only too quickly are
trivial, universal and eternally recurrent. Lumbago – or as
it is now more fashionably known, a 'slipped disc' –
accounts for more casualties than anything else. It is nearly
always contracted during the weekend previous to the
match concerned. It is contracted while swimming, playing squash, moving house, picking apples, digging the garden, amusing the children or trying to get upstairs without
waking the household.

Unforeseen family events come second on the list. These
are of a most appalling variety ranging from having to take
the dog to the vet; to a no-longer-postponable promise to
drive down to the New Forest to see the wife's mother; or
the children have measles (as if you'd ever asked *them* to
play for you); or everybody has to be taken to the South
of France for three weeks – a long-standing engagement
of which the Organizer is informed only a couple of days
before the match is due to take place.

Work, while it does not affect the majority of Coarse

Cricket Organizers in their efforts at team-gathering, most
certainly has unexpected results when (as in the case of the
author), your team is drawn largely from the entertain-
ment and medical professions. To include a doctor or two
in your side is always a good idea, as I will show in a
moment; but they tend to be the Bad Risks as far as your
team-building is concerned. Far too often their weekends
(and your carefully balanced side) are upset by an un-
scheduled demand on their services at the Hospital, and
when your doctor-members are South Africans you not
only lose the use of a car but also the advantage of players
who, almost without exception and regardless of their
talent for other aspects of cricket, never fail to hold any
catch that comes their way.

It is not enough, in drawing up your list of seventeen
possible players for the next match, merely to write down
the names of seventeen people who are good company and
good Coarse Cricketers. Cricket ability plays a part, of
course, and it is advisable in getting your team together
to ensure that it includes a reasonable proportion of batsmen and bowlers. But seventeen of the world's greatest
Test Match players would be useless to you in a Coarse
Cricket side without some means of getting them all there.
It is absolutely imperative at all stages of team-collecting
to see that there are enough cars to go round. A mediocre
player with room for three passengers in his car is of more
value to the Organizer than four England players without
a car between them.

A doctor with a car performs two useful functions: he
contributes materially to the solution of the transport problem and he is invaluable in his professional capacity in
tending the sick and wounded on your side and in advising

slightly injured opponents that, in their own interest, they should take no further part in the match. As a typical instance of the effect of a medical opinion in the course of a game I recall an occasion when, playing against the village of Great Missenden, Michael Shepley was discreet enough to avoid the risk of being absent from the run of 'The Chiltern Hundreds' and ducked a fierce bumper from a bowler who was beginning to play havoc with our innings. As a result of Mr Shepley's inspired evasive action the ball laid out the wicket-keeper, cutting his forehead open. The unfortunate fellow bled profusely and it was the unanimous and immediate opinion of the three young South African Fellows of the Royal College of Surgeons in our side that he should be taken at once to Amersham Hospital to have stitches put in the wound. Before the wicket-keeper could protest he was driven away in a car by one of our surgeons himself. This meant, of course, that a deputy wicket-keeper had to take over. The Great Missenden captain was the only available substitute, and being the captain his first action from behind the stumps was to take the dangerous bowler off. Michael Shepley's subsequent total of three runs has been known to this day as the Chiltern Hundred, for his innings, played as it was in a bowl of the Chiltern Hills, was as valuable as any century and enabled us to win the match by seven wickets (13-a-side).

In the course of collecting seventeen to come Sunday the Organizer may have to depute some of the team-building to members of the side who have accepted the invitation and also to members who have not. For the true Coarse Cricketer who is unable to play is nearly always able to find a deputy and will usually, when regretting his own inability to play, recommend one without being asked. Few Coarse Cricketers envy the Organizer his job but there is none who will not show constructive and practical sympathy for him in his sufferings.

There are few phrases in the world more gladdening to the aching heart of the Coarse Cricket Organizer than the words spoken over the telephone late on Saturday night: 'Are you still short for tomorrow? Because if you are I'll bring a chap called Finch Noyes along. He used to play for—' But the Organizer does not wait to learn of Mr Finch Noyes' qualifications; a player has been plucked out of the blue at a desperate moment, and that is all that matters. Besides, all newcomers to any Coarse Cricket side always have the same qualifications: 'I haven't played for years, of course . . .'

While the ultimate responsibility for the organization of a Coarse Cricket team rests with the Organizer, his administrative genius in planning and co-ordinating the unplannable and unco-ordinatable would be useless without the co-operation and initiative of members of his side. No Organizer can possibly be in the saloon bars of half a dozen London public houses at the same time on a Friday evening, looking for potential players whom nobody has seen for a week and whose lodgings in Bloomsbury, South Kensington, Bayswater and Fulham are still virgin territory to the Post Office Telephones service. He has to delegate to members this vital form of detective work, and it says much for the dogged and thorough methods of these amateur sleuths that their quarry rarely eludes them. Even the most inaccessible, untraceable Coarse Cricketer is a creature of at least one habit, and that is the habit of visiting a certain pub regularly. Once you have learned where and when he indulges in that habit, you can be fairly sure to find him. Most Organizers will find that this division of labour works well and it is seldom that a confident assurance that David will be in the Scarsdale on Friday evening fails to result in David's being at the match on Sunday. This selfless co-operation on the part of one's fellow-members is an expression of the team-spirit of which the game of Coarse Cricket is justifiably proud, for you will not find it very often in any other kind of cricket.

GETTING A TEAM TO THE MATCH. If all has gone well, then, breakfast time on Sunday morning should find you with as near to eleven players as you will ever get. For a moment on the previous afternoon it seemed as if the mystic number eleven was going to be achieved. You went to the Tavern at Lord's in a last-minute endeavour to add another player to the ten who had agreed to play for you. You found just the man for the job. A moment later you found just another man for the job, so you got him to come along too. But why, you may ask, if you were as sure as you could be of anything that you had a *full eleven*, why invite a twelfth man? The Organizer's answer to that could be

that all teams travel a twelfth man. But it would not be an honest answer. The wise Organizer knows that you can never have too many players; that if you have twelve in your side overnight, on Sunday morning not *one* player will suddenly drop out to leave you with eleven, but *two* players – leaving you with ten and one to borrow when you get there. The number eleven is the crock of gold of Coarse Cricket.

From an early hour on Sunday morning the Organizer's telephone starts ringing. Each time he picks it up he does so with a prayer on his lips – a prayer that the caller has nothing to do with the cricket, or if he has that he is not ringing to say that he cannot play after all, but that he wants to know how to get there or can somebody give him a lift as his car has broken down.

We will not deal with the matter of the caller who cannot play. It is too late to do anything now, and you will have to rely on the surplus male population of the village

to bring the side up to strength. But the question of transport is one to be prepared for; it is a subject which will have been the astute Organizer's constant pre-occupation all along, which – as I have suggested – will have influenced him more than anything else in the collection of his team.

The last-minute loss of an acceptor hitherto regarded as an absolutely certain runner can be disappointing enough at any time; but to lose a player *with a car*, on whom you were relying for the transportation of at least three other players, is perhaps the worst thing that can happen to any Organizer. If, in my own experience, there has never been an instance of complete failure to get players to a match, it has often been a close thing. In the end, when all else fails, there is such a thing as Public Transport. This, however, not only entails looking things up in a timetable which, the Organizer discovers, was liable to alteration without notice even when first printed in December, 1944, but also reveals the fact that the Lord's Day Observance Society is unashamedly Continental in its attitude towards the Sabbath compared with the British Railways system.

During the war, of course, most Coarse Cricket had to be reached by train and bus (which is why you have bought no A.B.C. since 1944), and it was surprising how many people grew used to the idea; and how quickly, too, they learned to leave the smart cricket bag at home and travel instead with a small, light suitcase or rucksack containing only the bare essentials of equipment, carrying a bat under the arm, perhaps, but relying on their cricket hosts to provide them with pads. This wartime habit, incidentally, led to open and general recognition of a practice that had long been instinctive in the true Coarse Cricketer: the borrowing of bats, pads and gloves from the other side. This aspect of the Coarse Cricketer's craft, however, will be more fully discussed in the section on Costume and Equipment.

Assuming, however, that thanks to the Organizer's initiative and genius for improvisation and the imaginative co-operation of members, a team can be got to The Match at all, it is of the utmost importance to consider the E.T.S. – Estimated Time of Starting. This, both in practice and the mind of the experienced Organizer, will be as elastic and unpredictable as the E.T.A., for the Estimated Time of Arrival is by custom never more precisely defined than being 'somewhere about opening time'.

Whereas, however, an early E.T.A. has many obvious and desirable advantages, an early E.T.S. is to be resisted at all costs. Although there can be very few Organizers in whom such resistance is not instinct, it might be as well to set down the reasons why a newcomer to the Organization of Coarse Cricket should not be too anxious to demur literally to the opposition's request for a 2.30 start. Unless such an invitation is interpreted as meaning '2.30 for 3 p.m.' (if not later) the whole tenor, tempo and temper of a Coarse Cricket match will be most disastrously upset.

Let us analyse the implications of a formal 2.30 p.m. as the E.T.S. To be changed and ready to take the field at that time without having violent indigestion through bolting your food means beginning luncheon not later than 1.15 p.m.; which means that in order to enjoy the traditional, unhurried session of social reunion and refreshment preceding the luncheon or barside sandwiches the E.T.A. at The Local must be not more than a very few minutes after Sunday opening time, 12 noon; which means that you will have had no time to dawdle on your way down, to stretch your legs for your first drink at any of

the seductive-looking pubs *en route*; which means you had
to drive at breakneck speed to keep your E.T.A., or had to
rise at an unchristian hour to drive at a sensible speed; all
of which is alien to the whole spirit of Coarse Cricket.

The moral effect on The Team of a comfortably
achieved E.T.S. will be obvious; its effect on the opposition can be devastating. I recall an occasion when a fixture
with a Sussex village was scheduled to begin at the unlikely hour of 1.30 p.m. on a Sunday (we discovered this
only upon arriving for our customary 3 o'clock start). By
the time we arrived the opposition, who had been changed
into flannels for nearly two hours, had virtually tired themselves out with a good eighty minutes of 'knocking-up';
and – which was even more important – the local village
band, specially engaged for the occasion, had exhausted
its breath and its repertoire long before our arrival. The
absence of moral support from the band was clearly noticeable, for in place of the stirring martial music obviously
planned to inspire and encourage the village team (wicket-
keeper: 'Tich' Cornford, Sussex and England), the best
the band could do during the afternoon was to play a
languorous version of 'Moonlight and Roses', repeated
at twenty-minute intervals, the soporific effect of which
was to cause much careless play by our opponents.

The early E.T.S., then, is not only to be avoided, but
will be found to be impossible. This means that, with no
effort on their part, a Coarse Cricket side automatically
gains a strong tactical advantage before a ball has been
bowled. The slightest effort, indeed, to achieve anything but
a normal E.T.S. puts the team at a disadvantage at once;
it prolongs hours of play, makes everybody bad tempered
and spoils the social side of a summer's day in the country.

3. Technique

BATTING. In studying the technical aspects of Coarse Cricket, *how* to play it, as distinct from *when, where* and *why* to play it, much that follows in the course of this chapter will be of considerable retrospective assistance to the Organizer faced with the initial problem of *Getting a Team Together*. Which is a gentle way of suggesting that whatever the Organizer's team may look like on paper on a Saturday night, he doesn't know the half of it until the fateful hour of the E.T.S. has struck on Sunday afternoon.

Whether his team consists of seven or thirteen players, the Organizer will discover the moment he takes up a pencil to write down a batting order that, with the exception of himself, everybody on the side is a born Number Seven. To accept this without a struggle (which is what everybody concerned expects you to do) is bad for morale and tends to undermine what little authority you may have over The Team. Also, it makes the score book look pretty ridiculous if the spaces for batsmen Nos. 1–6 and 8–11 are left entirely blank, although, heaven knows, even if the entire team bats at No. 7 it is unlikely that they will score enough runs between them to do more than make an ugly smudge on that part of the page.

The Organizer, who, now that he has reached the field of play and may therefore freely declare a State of Emergency shall hereinafter be referred to as The Captain, will discover that there are several ways in which to deal with this situation. The first is to ignore all protests and present the team with a *fait accompli* in the form of a batting list against which there is no appeal. This stern, dictatorial method has been known to work wonders; not that the order of batting is adhered to, or anything like it, but because, having had his last say in the matter, the Captain can then leave the players to sort it all out among themselves. And it is surprising how, after much argument and wrangling between individuals, quite a reasonable batting order will result from this.

One position in the batting order, however, must be regarded as completely sacrosanct, and that is the last place of all. This, since time immemorial, has always been the Captain's exclusive property; it gives him repeated opportunities to play a Captain's Innings, and if he fails in this (which is more than likely) then he is spared the humiliation of a lonely walk back from the crease and the ignominy of a very noticeable 'O' on the score board. By going in last the Captain is able to return to the pavilion in company, for at the fall of the last wicket he will be accompanied by his fellow batsman, two umpires, and eleven or more fielders. Also, if by some mischance his partner should lose his wicket, then the Captain's unfinished innings will help his batting average considerably, but he must take care (as if he could help it) to get out at least once during the season otherwise he will not be able to work out his average, if any.

One result of the democratic system of a batting order sorted out by the players themselves is that (with the exception of the Captain himself) there is rarely any question of its being the expression of an order of merit. Lacking as it does the influence of a single co-ordinating mind it tends to be a pretty haphazard affair, but very often the effect can be most satisfactory. Thus, on one occasion, when no fewer than five of my natural-born Number Sevens scrambled for places as low down in the batting order as possible, an opposition ignorant of our domestic ways was lulled into a false sense of security, only to discover that, as the *Saffron Walden Weekly News* later so rightly described us, we were 'a side without a tail'.

In so far as the Captain has any influence on the batting order at all the question of a pair of openers is best solved by sending in a couple of purely defensive batsmen. (A great deal of flattery, cajolery, bribery and appealing to The Sporting Spirit is necessary to get a pair of openers

to the crease but with patience and a little moral support
from the rest of the team it can be done in the end.) The
purpose of selecting defensive instead of attacking batsmen
as an opening pair is moral and tactical, for one of the
most powerful moral and tactical weapons possessed by a
Coarse Cricket team is that of being able to *bore* the
opposition into mistakes.

A safe, slow-scoring opening pair will try the patience
of any village captain after a time, and he will change his
bowling. First and second change bowlers are rarely so
alarming as the opening couple, who are inevitably aggressive and demonic unless worn down, so that in practice
a mere 20 runs on the board by the first change of bowling
can be worth all of 50 or 60 to the side in the circumstances.

How you find your safe, opening defensive batsmen is
another matter, of course; but in the initial stages of
Collecting a Team it is always wise to bespeak one or two
players who have recently been at a Good School. If they
are *still* at a Good School, so much the better, for in all
forms of Coarse Cricket the schoolboy batsman proves to
be an almost immovable object. It is always better, therefore, to have a schoolboy on your side; when he is on the
other side he tends to retire when he has made a hundred
and to congratulate you on your best yorker which, need-
less to say, he stops with the greatest of ease.

For the rest of the question of the batting order, the
Captain must ruthlessly assert his authority and give
priority to any claimant to the position of Number Seven
who is a golf Blue or a hockey international. To golf Blues
a cricket ball is the size of a balloon, even when in motion;
while to a hockey international, batting is so much less

dangerous than playing hockey that he will revel in a ball-game so relatively free of physical hazards. It is rarely that a golfer or hockey player fails to score freely in these circumstances.

All in all, batting must be regarded as the most difficult aspect of Coarse Cricket, principally because there is little opportunity for a batsman to develop his technique. If he is out first ball he is out until the next match, by which time he will by no possible chance have had a net and so begins his next innings in the same unpractised state in which he ended his last innings.

In collecting a team a Captain should always aim at a preponderance of batsmen over bowlers. Even with a weak bowling side one may count on a reasonable chance of dismissing the opposition sooner or later, if only thanks to batting mistakes caused by over-confidence. The opposition, however, never seems to make comparable bowling or fielding mistakes and the accumulation of runs is consequently depressing uphill work from the start and a constant cause of anxiety to the Captain, particularly when

his side is batting last. (The advantages of batting last are nevertheless considerable and will be discussed in a later section.)

Once – by whatever means – a batting order has been arranged, the Captain should not hesitate to improvise at a moment's notice during the course of the innings. He will find little difficulty in persuading his Number Eight to go in at the fall of the fourth wicket if, in the Captain's opinion, that batsman is likely to flourish at the expense of the bowler then in action. He may, however, have some trouble with that Old Harrovian with a weakness for gin, but experience and psychology will enable him to decide on the right moment to send him in to bat – the moment before carefree confidence degenerates into comatose indifference. It is surprising, in such circumstances, to note how deeply rooted in the subconscious mind a sound early cricket education can be, and how many times your Old Harrovian will come to the rescue with perfect cover drives which he will afterwards be astonished to learn he was able to make at all.

If there is one final thing to be said about Batting it is that the Captain should early in the season impress upon his regular players the need for them to enlarge their circle of friends to include batsmen, rather than bowlers, who need a game on Sunday. In Coarse Cricket the bowling can look after itself – up to a point. A team is always full of potential bowlers; it is never full of potential batsmen, and you can never include too many in the side.

BOWLING. It is one of the irrefutable axioms of Coarse Cricket that the bad balls take more wickets than the good ones, and it is for this reason that the Captain can and must regard every member of his side as a bowling asset. However out of practice a bowler may be he cannot be taken off until he has completed the over, and during the course of those six balls a sufficiently high proportion of them may pitch on the ground to encourage the Captain to keep him on. It is in this opportunity to find something approaching a length that the bowler has the advantage over the batsman every time; the batsman who loses his wicket has no chance to redeem himself, whereas the bowler whose first ball is knocked out of the ground has another five balls (and an unlimited number of wides and no-balls to play with before he is taken off, and even then he can always be brought back again).

When it comes to the strategic disposition of his forces the Captain will find bowlers a very different kettle of fish from the batsmen. He will encounter none of that infuriating reluctance to perform which characterized his attempts to arrange a batting order; no bowler will ever admit (let alone insist) that he is 'a born Fourth Change'. Everybody, on the contrary, wants to open the bowling at once.

In such circumstances, of course, the democratic method which was more or less successful in sorting out the batting order cannot be applied. The Captain must assume the role of dictator and if he is a bowler himself (and the surest way of the Captain enjoying his Coarse Cricket to the full is to be a bowler) then one half of the question as to who opens the bowling is answered. The other half is best answered by earmarking early on in the process of Getting a Team Together, at least one player whose natural *métier* is that of a bowler.

The 'career bowler', however, must be selected for more than just his ability to keep a length and hit the stumps. He must be selected, above all, for his temperament and whole-hearted acceptance of the principles and traditions of Coarse Cricket. And one of the first principles to accept as a bowler is that it is almost impossible to set a conventional field against a village side; if he expects his outswinger to end up safely in the hands of cover point he will soon learn that what he really needs is another man on the square leg boundary. The other problems which confront the bowler in Coarse Cricket will be discussed more fully in the section on Fielding.

Meanwhile, let it be noted that in Coarse Cricket things tend to go in opposites. Particularly bowling. It is the opposition's opening fast bowlers who most usually get your batsmen's wickets. This is because your batsmen are almost inevitably old and grey and full of sleep and no longer able to see the ball on to the bat. As they put it themselves with a masterly touch of understatement: they lack match practice.

The opposition's batsmen, on the other hand, seem to revel in your opening bowlers, and the faster and more accurately aggressive the bowling the more they enjoy the experience. They miss the balls they should snick to first slip and drive over the head of mid-on those which should bowl them neck and crop.

Your batsmen will welcome a slow bowler; the opposition's will be helplessly at sea with him.

It is therefore of the utmost importance to include in your team a slow leg-break bowler. Because it is the ambition of every country boy to bowl faster than the next, the art of slow bowling is scarcely known in English village cricket. The wise Captain who exploits this fact to the full will be amply rewarded – by a harvest of stumpings, catches at silly first slip and, if the bowler makes the best use of the sun behind him at the south-western end of a pitch running S.W. to N.E. and pitches the ball very high

into the air, by the gratifying sound of shattered stumps and falling bails. Even if the ball with the sun behind it is visible on its journey towards the batsman, the slow speed at which it travels through the air is usually more than the batsman's patience can tolerate. He will make his stroke far too soon, and if he hits it at all it will most likely result in an easy caught-and-bowled.

It may well be argued that if the slow leg-break bowler is such a success in a Coarse Cricket side and such a comfort to the Captain, the most sensible and obvious thing to do would be to *open* the bowling with him, keeping the more conventional opening pace-bowlers to deal with the opposition's tail, if any. On reflection there seems to be no earthly reason why this should not be done; if it is 'not cricket', then it is high time it was. Unfortunately, there is in even the coarsest of Coarse Cricketers that streak of bourgeois cowardice and respectability found in most revolutionaries which will cause him to hesitate at the prospect of questioning the validity of one of the unshakable Canons of Cricket: that one does not open the bowling with a slow bowler. It is a pity, but there it is; you can't monkey with human nature.

For the rest, the Captain will leave his bowlers to their own devices. It is useless for him to instruct them in how and when to unleash the two most effective and devastating balls known in Coarse Cricket: the full toss that swings from leg to hit the top of the off stump, and the 'bouncer' which pitches (the first time) a couple of yards in front of the bowler and ends up (on the second bounce) as a yorker hitting the base of the middle stump. Such balls, so fortunately unpredictable, cannot be delivered on request. They just happen.

FIELDING. The Captain's first introduction to the question of fielding will occur as he leads his side out on to the field. He will note that he has made no provision for a wicket-keeper.

The principles which govern the creation of a batting order and the bowling rota cannot, unfortunately, be applied to the matter of the wicket-keeper. The Captain cannot apply the democratic method of letting his team sort it all out among themselves, as he can when his side has to bat. Nor can he be dictatorial and appoint a wicket-keeper, as he can appoint an opening bowler; equally, he will not find his players clamouring anxiously to keep wicket with the same enthusiasm as they demand to be allowed to bowl.

There is only one thing the Captain can do: ask, with a note of pathos in the voice which will come naturally, whether there is anybody among those gathered together who can *possibly* keep wicket.

Such is the glory and uncertainty of Coarse Cricket that there is always one fearless member of the side who will volunteer to take over the most dangerous position known to man. He will – understandably – make his offer timidly and modestly: 'I haven't done it for years, of course; but I'll have a shot . . .'

You, for your part, could hardly care less if he had never done it before at all. You have found somebody willing to keep wicket and who, if he does not save many runs, has at least saved the appearance of the side. You will soon learn the extent of his previous experience when setting the field for the first over, a stage in the game which will be reached only after some delay caused by your wicket-keeper having to return to the pavilion and borrow the necessary pads and gloves from the opposition.

If, when your wicket-keeper is finally rigged out and on the field, he looks anxiously over his shoulder as he prepares to take up his position behind the stumps, signal your fine-leg to stand a little finer. This will give your wicket-keeper confidence and provide him with the security of a long-stop without the indignity of calling the fieldsman by that name. Although why the time-honoured position of long-stop should be so looked down upon these days I do not know, for his existence is essential to all forms of Coarse Cricket. Not only does he give moral support to the wicket-keeper, save byes and overthrows and retrieve wides, but his presence is frequently forgotten by the opposition batsmen, with the result that they learn too late that a ball which beats the wicket-keeper is not a certain bye but a likely run-out. The position of long-stop, indeed, is not to be regarded lightly; it is no position in which to 'hide' an indifferent fielder, for he needs a sense of positioning, a safe pair of hands and considerable agility. He is as indispensable to the side with an expert wicket-keeper as to one with a stumper who has merely donned pads and gloves to oblige. The only real trouble seems to be the title the fieldsman is given; if the name 'long-stop' is too reminiscent of cricket on the sands for some people, 'fine-leg', while a sop to the wicket-keeper's *amour propre*, is at once a little too euphemistic to describe a long-stop's function and inadequate to describe what the position is in practice: a combination of both positions. Perhaps some name like 'deep-wicket' would cover it, but even so it does not quite suggest the 'roving' nature of the job.

The player at 'deep-wicket' may be confidently relied

upon to cope with the on-side behind the wicket. The off-side can be left to the familiar position of deep third-man, standing about the same distance from the wicket-keeper as deep-wicket. The experienced Captain will have a deep third-man for *all* his bowlers, and he will choose him as he would a deep-field: for his ability to hold high catches. This may seem an unnecessary qualification in a third-man to those whose experience of cricket is confined to the academic study of the game; but not in Coarse Cricket, it isn't. More mighty off-drives in Coarse Cricket end up as catches in the hands of deep-third man than anywhere else on the field, and they are sent there by strokes off fast bowlers and slow bowlers alike.

Apart from acting occasionally as an off-side deep-wicket and retrieving the balls snicked between first slip and the wicket-keeper (which the wicket-keeper will never consider to have been a possible catch as it clearly came off the batsman's foot and was a leg-bye), deep third-man will have comparatively little ground-fielding to do. The late cut is a stroke not often attempted in Coarse Cricket, though from time to time a defensive forward stroke will have exactly the same effect.

When the bowling changes ends at the end of the over neither deep-wicket nor deep third-man need move a yard, for they will both be ideally placed to take over the positions of rather deep long-mid-off and rather deep long-mid-on respectively, the original occupants of these last two places now, of course, taking over as deep-wicket and deep third-man respectively. This all saves a lot of walking about and changing over.

The principal duties of rather deep long-mid-off and rather deep long-mid-on are, first, to patrol the boundary

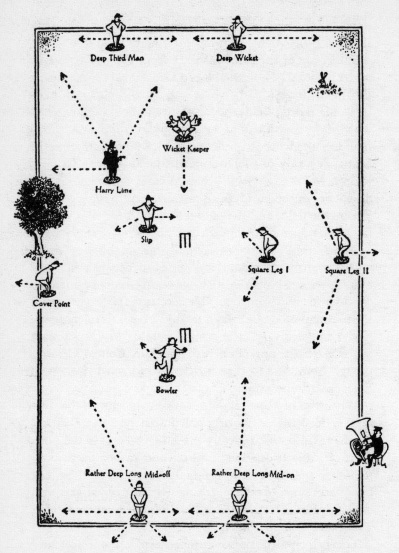

Field set for Slow Bowler

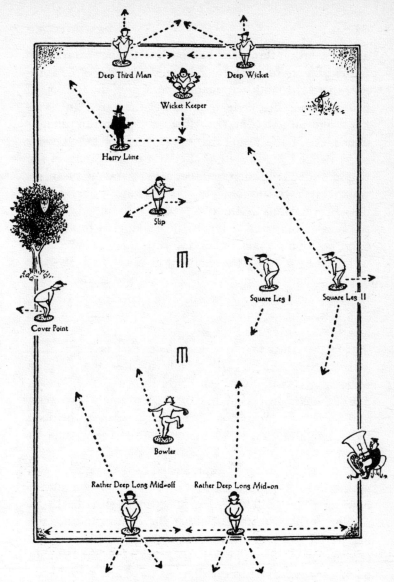

Field set for Fast Bowler

and, second, to throw the ball back to the bowler when it
passes him out of reach (which is nearly always). In addition these two mid-long fielders must give the illusion of
fielding much nearer in than in fact they are. Unless he
has a mid-off and a mid-on close beside him (an ostenta-
tious piece of affectation that never comes off) the bowler
must depend on the *moral* effect on the batsman of the
two mid-long fieldsmen to discourage the taking of singles
which – it is quite obvious – are always 'there'. This
illusion is created by the two fielders standing close in as
the bowler prepares to bowl and walking *backwards* to a
safer position as he makes his run up – a movement
which is the exact opposite of that favoured in fancy-class
cricket, where the fielders always move *in* as the bowler
runs up.

If it is at all possible it is always best to aim at having
four South Africans in the key positions under discussion,
for whether their favoured game is cricket or rugby they
all seem to be able to catch a ball. In all the many games
I have played with South Africans I have only ever known
one of them to drop a catch. Paul was extremely apologetic
and very angry; he not only dropped a catch in the deep
but his cigarette on to his flannels and burned a hole in
them.

The Captain, already experienced in the matter of dis-
posing batsmen into a batting order and bowlers into a
bowling order, will find that in setting a field he has a
similar problem to face. Neither the democratic nor the
dictatorial method will work in setting a field; only the
personal and polite approach will ever enable him to avoid
having seven players in the slips. As there are 'born Number Sevens', so there are always an embarrassing number

of players on the side who are born slip-fielders. It is therefore fatal ever to *ask* anybody where they would like to
field; the only way is to *request* with a maximum of diffi-
dence that they should fill one of the far-too-many wide
open spaces in the field. All protestations and individual
preferences should be ignored, particularly of those players
well into middle age who complain that they are no longer
young and agile enough to field in front of the wicket. It is
precisely the ageing and unagile fielders who are most use
in front of the wicket, for their reflexes are slow and they
are no longer able to side-step with ease the hard drive
coming straight towards them. Use younger fielders, by all
means, where there is likely to be much chasing after the
ball to be done, but the good solid, middle-aged shin is a
noble sacrifice on the altar of thwarted boundaries, and its
bruises – apart from being something to show everybody
for a week afterwards – are never acquired in vain. They
are cricket's medals awarded by Nature for grit and courage.

The greatest possible use should always be made of the
shadows cast by trees and buildings around the field of
play. A cover-point fielding on the boundary in the shade
of a tree under which spectators are seated will be almost
invisible to the batsman, and many a run-out has resulted
from a smart return by a camouflaged cover-point whose
presumed non-existence has encouraged batsmen to take
a leisurely second run. If the batsman is not run out the
rate of scoring will nevertheless slacken in that part of the
field once cover-point's presence has been noted. The fact
that there was always time for a *smartly run* two off the
ball hit towards the far-flung fieldsman does not occur to
the batsman; he will not risk more than a quick single
next time.

The Captain himself, when he is not bowling (which is seldom), has one position on the field which is his exclusively by traditional right – mid-off. (During his bowling spell, of course, he will field between overs at first slip in the conventional manner.) The advantages of this position are many. It is rare in Coarse Cricket to encounter a batsman who is intentionally strong on the off side, and such balls as ever come in the direction of mid-off come either as a trickle from a defensive stroke, or as high dolly catches which arrive so slowly that the bowler would have plenty of time to make a catch-and-bowled himself, but which the Captain, setting an example to his men, will misguidedly try to hold instead. As a Coarse Cricket Captain of many years experience I have rather inclined in recent times to leave these catches to the bowler. In a moment of over-zealous example-setting a few seasons ago I chased after one of these skiers from mid-off, collided with the wicket-keeper and fractured my jaw in several places. If one *must* break one's jaw at cricket then I chose the right occasion, for our opponents were Guy's Hospital Coarse Cricket Team who drove me back to their hospital in due course where I was an in- and out-patient for several weeks afterwards.

Another advantage of the position of mid-off is the comparative freedom enjoyed by the fielder from natural hazards. Even on the more modestly mown grounds where Coarse Cricket is played the position is always on the 'square'; consequently, the ball travels towards you across even ground, and if you keep your feet apart in fielding the ball there is little likelihood of its getting up and hitting you in the face. The rest of your side, fielding in the rough, may be exposed to many other dangers, such as hoof-marks, rabbit holes, cows, ponies and their by-products; but it must be pointed out that because of these natural features of the ground the velocity of the ball is considerably reduced. But even if the ball does kick up and hit them on the person, it is surely not unreasonable that the Captain should be spared these risks. What general, after all, lives under exactly the same conditions as the men he commands?

The answer is: the Captain of a Coarse Cricket Team, only more so.

CAPTAINCY. The position, rank and occupation of Captain involves him who undertakes it in more than the accomplishment of those tasks discussed so far. While he may be batsman, bowler and fieldsman for no more than an afternoon at a time, he is the Captain throughout the year, summer and winter, on and off the field.

Leaving aside those headaches to do with Organization, the position of Captain demands of its occupant many gifts not usually associated with any known sport. We hear a great deal of the ambassadorial qualifications demanded of a captain appointed by the M.C.C. to lead a team in Australia. He is expected to make speeches, listen to speeches, get his team to bed early, keep sober and be polite to the Press. His contact with the opposition is virtually confined to tossing up, getting them out and making runs against them; and explaining why to the Press.

But no captain of an M.C.C. touring side is ever faced at Perth, for instance, with the stern looks which greet the arrival of a Coarse Cricket team at the scene of the match. One never heard, for instance, of Sir Leonard Hutton or Mr P. B. H. May being asked why they were so late arriving from London, nor of them apologizing for being four or five players short. The Captain of a Coarse Cricket side, on the other hand, is regularly having to talk himself out of these and other situations.

Once he has made up his mind what he is going to say, the Captain can safely stick to his prepared speech and trot it out match after match. There are two ways of dealing with the question of being late. The first is to take the initiative and say to the opposition captain with bewildered humility: 'I'm so sorry we're so late, but it was farther than we thought.' This line rarely fails to inspire forgiveness, even though the fixture has been played twice a year for the past fifteen years or more.

The second method, to be employed when the opposition has spoken first, is to adopt a hearty manner and slapping the complainant on the back cry laughingly: 'It's all very well for *you*, old man, you *live* here. We've come very nearly forty miles this morning.' This will lead to general laughter and drinks all round – at the Captain's expense.

More serious, however, is the matter of arriving short of four or five players. In this case the Captain not only has to apologize for a breakdown in organization, but in the same breath has to plead with the opposition to help him out. Coarse Cricket being what it is nobody really thinks any the less of you for turning up with too few players, but it is as well to take the initiative and get your two-pennorth in first.

'I'm afraid,' you say, hesitantly, 'I'm afraid we may be one or two short.' 'May be?' You know damn well you're not likely to have more than seven players all told, and you've known it for the past forty-eight hours and more; but your diffident understatement suggests that you have tried hard (which heaven knows you have) and that your failure, if not an Act of God, has been in the face of the greatest odds. Your explanations of such large-scale absenteeism need never depart from the truth: your players couldn't make it, for one or other of the reasons mentioned in the section on *Getting a Team Together*.

While you yourself, as Captain and Organizer, may feel a little ashamed at the modest dimensions of your turn-out and perhaps a little depressed by the absence of several of your better players, there is no need to despair of getting a game of cricket. Local loyalty is never so strong that recruits cannot be found to play against the village; nor, on the rare occasions when you arrive with too many players, will any of them hesitate to opt out and play against you. It is The Game which counts above all things with true Coarse Cricketers, no matter how or where they find it.

In fancy-class cricket one of the first duties of the Captain is to win the toss. It is the same in Coarse Cricket, but with this difference: in a vast majority of cases whichever side wins the toss the result, as far as you are concerned, will be the same. You will field first.

The idea of fielding first is, of course, contrary to all the known principles of cricket as it is generally played. But in Coarse Cricket the known principles of the game do not always apply. There are many valid reasons why it is better to field first than to bat first, and the Captain who can win the toss and thus make assurance doubly sure is in a position to thrust home a number of advantages not apparent to those unversed in the subtleties of Coarse Cricket.

Firstly, by fielding first, you have the use of what is likely to be the only new ball in the match. You may have to supply the ball yourself but the cost is well worth it.

Secondly, it is better to have your side emerge from its post-prandial stupor when it is fielding than when it is batting.

Thirdly, it is a great moral advantage to know, when you come to bat, how many runs are needed for victory. Not only is a possible defeat by x runs less humiliating on paper than a defeat by x wickets, but the incentive to score is greater when you know what you're up against than when you are batting merely to make a total which may or may not be adequate.

Fourthly, the side that bats last has control over the clock. As the time approaches for the drawing of stumps (6.55 p.m. and not a moment later on Sundays) the batting side can decide whether to play for a dishonourable draw, or, if victory is in sight, to have a bash, or, if defeat is inevitable, to go down with wickets flying in all directions. In any case, you are in a position of being able to finish the game sharp at 6.55 p.m., whereas if the opposition are batting you are completely at their mercy and you may find yourself capering around the field long after opening time while they hit off the necessary runs or one of their batsmen completes his fifty. It is one of the curiosities of Coarse Cricket that while your side is always willing to admit a moral defeat the opposition is strangely reluctant as a rule to accept a moral victory. It is therefore highly important to bat second and so exploit the fact that you are guests and can pack up when you want to; you have – you must remind your hosts – to drive back to London and you don't want to be too late.

Once you have lost the toss a few times against the same opposition and noted that they prefer to bat first, the formality of tossing up can be dispensed with altogether. In my own case this agreement was reached many years ago with the thrice-yearly fixtures against the village of Great Missenden. It makes for universal satisfaction.

The Captain who is a bowler, and he will get the maximum enjoyment out of his Coarse Cricket if he is, may find himself having to cope with situations and behaviour which the batsman-captain does not usually encounter in the ordinary course of business. The Captain who, being a bowler, does not keep himself on until he can no longer run up to the wicket to bowl, can hardly be considered a natural Coarse Cricketer. With a democratically-inclined concern such as his team there will naturally be considerable vocal criticism of his action, but the experienced Captain will long ago have learned to treat it with equanimity. The worst that can happen is for the fielders to go on a lie-down strike.

The Captain who has not known this situation before may well view with alarm the sight of his entire side lying full length on the grass as he prepares to bowl. Believing that the game cannot continue without the full co-operation of his fielders, he may plead with them to get up and behave. He will probably do so in vain, for strikers cannot be reasoned with and arbitration is a lengthy business. The umpires are pretty powerless, too, for as far as I know there is nothing in the laws of Cricket to force a recumbent fielder to stand on his feet again. 'Unfair play' might cover it, but to whom is the play unfair? Not to the opposition; only to the Captain of the fielders' own side, and he can hardly ask the umpires to help him in his effort to maintain discipline among his own players. Perhaps it is possible to adapt the Law concerning the two-minute limit which, if it is exceeded, causes the dallying in-going batsman to forfeit his innings; but unfortunately that particular Law cannot be held to cover the fielding side. Besides, what could the fielding side forfeit for non-participation or, at any rate, delaying tactics on the field? If they refuse to take part, the worst that could happen would be that the match would be awarded to the batting side by the umpires. And the batting side, one thinks, would hardly consider that a very satisfactory conclusion to the day's fixture; the fact that your side has protested against your bowling suggests that the batting side are in a fairly happy and flourishing position, while the fielding side will barely be perturbed at the thought of not batting since so long as the Captain keeps himself on there appears to them little likelihood of their getting an innings anyway.

There is, however, one simple, devastating and infallible weapon possessed by the Captain. All he has to do is to continue to bowl. As soon as the ball is anywhere near the batsman the effect will be immediate and magical. Your lie-down strikers will scramble to their feet in panic and sheer self-protection, for the fielder has not yet been born who can calmly lie on the grass, not knowing how or when the ball is going to be hit in his direction. Try it and see for yourself.

The success of this simple psychological ruse will have a stimulating moral effect on the Captain and he will probably silence all criticism by taking a much needed wicket before the end of the interrupted over. And when he does (or even if he doesn't) he can then take himself off with a magnanimous gesture, forgiving those who trespassed against him and letting them know that the gesture has absolutely nothing to do with their unruly behaviour.

That other pretty habit of the modern worker, Working To Rule, has not, so far as I know, yet been applied to Coarse Cricket. I have often wished it could be. It would have a most welcome salutary effect on the proficiency of your team's cricket.

Reverting, in conclusion, to Captaincy off the field, the Captain will, of course, remember to bring a cheque book with him; although he is the guest of the opposition he will find that the eventual cost of entertaining the day's opponents after the match will be far in excess of any loose cash he has brought with him. He must also make a point of keeping the landlord of the pub liberally supplied with drinks during the evening, firstly, as an insurance against his taking amiss any obstreperousness which some of your members may show and, secondly, in retribution for the good-natured but over-amorous behaviour after the previous match of one or two of the younger members of your side, who so far forgot themselves as to pinch the landlord's daughter of The Cricketers' backside.

This eventuality, as I suggested earlier on, demands

tactful handling by the Captain and the best approach (if you want the landlord to cash that cheque for you) is one of laughing boys-will-be-boys pleading, a not-too-ribald hint that if you were twenty years younger yourself no doubt you'd be tempted to do the same thing because Betty really *is* so pretty, and how glad you are to hear she is married as she'll obviously be an ideal wife to her husband. If the landlord, with your welfare at heart, points out a very large man in the corner as being Betty's husband, lose no time in warning your delinquent colleagues of the fact and suggest they'd better play a game of darts.

In practice, the Captain is not really held responsible for all the caprices and whims of his players before and after the match, but he will always *feel* he is. Even after a quarter of a century of Coarse Cricket I was never able to rid myself of this feeling. I suppose it is just one of the prices you pay for the folly of being Captain, a position which – once you have experienced it – you would not change for the captaincy of an England team that wins the Ashes.

4. Ethics and Customs

'*THE last time I played in a village match I was given out l.b.w. first ball. That sort of umpiring should be looked into.*'
—H.R.H. THE DUKE OF EDINBURGH.

In writing of the Ethics of Coarse Cricket, S. Hughes presents his compliments to S. Potter and humbly suggests that S. Potter's esteemed volume entitled *Gamesmanship* shows the practice and principles of that art to be elementary by comparison with the ethical practices and principles prevailing in the Art of Coarse Cricket.

Coarse Cricket is the essence of Gamesmanship and, indeed, may be considered to be the original ancestor of all sporting behaviour which isn't 'quite cricket'. It is curious to reflect, in passing, that the phrase 'it's not cricket' should derive from a game which, one can only infer, must have at some time or other inspired more skulduggerous and shady tactics than any other. 'At some time or other?' To the disinterested student of the Laws of Cricket the idea of the game setting itself up as being pure as the driven snow is cynical, ironical and presumptuous. Was there ever a game in which there were more underhand but strictly legal ways of defeating an opponent, where by subtle deception and false amiability an opponent can be removed from the battle by such ruses as inducing him to handle the ball, or to strike it twice, by the bowler whipping off the bails when a batsman is backing up? Just read the Laws of Cricket and ask yourself whether a great many of them are 'quite cricket'. It is seldom, of course, that these obscurer Laws are invoked, but the fact that they are Laws at all makes one a little suspicious of what kind of a game cricket really is.

As a bowler myself I have noticed with some shame and considerable relief that most of these rather reprehensible methods are directed against the batting side. The fielding side is not nearly so harshly done by. Apart from the bowler being forbidden to throw (throwing, in any case, is not so easy or effective as legitimate bowling, for how could any right-hander *throw* a leg-break?) and the fielder prohibited from stopping or catching the ball with his cap, shrimping net or shopping basket, there is nothing in the Laws governing fielding which approaches the restrictions imposed upon the batsmen.

Batsmen – like Sir Len Hutton, for instance – have actually been given out in a Test Match for obstructing the field, but there has never, so far as I know, been a case in any class of cricket of a fielder being removed for the rest of the innings for obstructing the batsman. And a very good thing too, for in Coarse Cricket, for example, many run-outs have been achieved by bowler, cover-point, first slip and rather deep long-mid-off all chasing after a ball on the on-side, crossing the paths of the running batsmen at care-fully calculated intervals and developing the resultant state of confusion by shouting 'All right, I'll go!' 'This end!' 'Other end!' and similar slogans, while square-leg runs towards the off-side of the bowler's end and rather deep long-mid-on scampers to prevent overthrows on the leg-side of the wicket-keeper. A combined operation of this nature can be made to look quite fair and it would have to be a shrewd umpire to recognize it as obstruction of the batsman, even if such a Law existed.

I suppose when the Laws were first made forbidding the batsman to handle the ball, hit it twice, and stand beyond his crease when he is at the bowler's end they were made with a purpose – to stop the batsman picking up the ball and throwing a six, hitting a stationary ball for four with a No. 2 iron shot, or standing 15 yards in front of the bowling crease. The mystery is why these Laws are still included, for their breach in each case makes the game of cricket more difficult and in the case of over-zealous backing up, dangerous as well. One would have thought these factors would act as automatic deterrents without having to set them down as what are, in practice, superfluous proscriptions. Certainly in Coarse Cricket, where the predominating instincts are self-preservation and anything for a quiet life, they are not recognized as Laws. They are simply Not Cricket, and as such do not exist either in the observance or the breach.

We who are Coarse Cricketers by nature pride ourselves on a complete lack of hypocrisy. Our ethical standards are maintained openly and honestly – well, maintained at any rate. We do not consider it 'quite cricket', for instance, to claim extra time in order to gain a victory. If at 6.55 p.m. six runs are needed with four wickets to fall, we draw stumps just the same. It is a relief to the opposition who are convinced they have avoided certain defeat, while for our part we are quite happy to have scored a moral victory which, if extra time had been played, might well have ended in losing by at least five runs.

I recall an occasion which proved the wisdom of this consistent view of the undesirability of extra time. At 6.55 p.m. we were 80 runs behind with six wickets to fall. It was generally agreed that an extra half hour would mean scoring at the prodigious rate of 160 runs per hour, and that therefore a draw was inevitable. What we carefully failed to suggest was that thirty minutes was ample time for the opposition to get us out for far fewer than 80 runs. As it was, the drawing of stumps at the normal time satisfied everybody concerned; the opposition and ourselves alike considering that we had had a narrow escape, although for quite different reasons.

Broadly speaking, anything that is not specifically contrary to the Laws of Cricket is permissible in Coarse Cricket, particularly when your side is fielding. Any fielder shall be permitted to smoke in the field, insofar as this is compatible with efficiency. No player, for instance, attempting to hold a catch in the deep field should do so with a cigarette in his hand (I have already cited an example of the folly of this in the section on *Fielding*); he must keep his hands entirely free by keeping the cigarette in his mouth or parking it temporarily on the grass.

The question of beer in the field is not quite so easy, although its presence should be encouraged on several grounds. The difficulty is to persuade your fielders that so far from their mugs of beer being in danger they will instinctively exert themselves to protect them. A pint glass placed on the grass between the legs will improve the player's ground fielding unrecognizably. On the approach of a ball along the ground he will automatically step in front of the glass, keeping his heels together as he fields the ball. If the ball slips through his legs and breaks the beer glass he will be more than extra careful next time. Even Coarse Cricketers learn from their mistakes.

A pint mug placed behind and touching the stumps at the bowler's and the striker's ends respectively is also calculated to have a beneficial effect on the fielding. The two glasses at once become absolutely irresistible targets for throwing in, for anybody who can score a direct hit on the target will almost certainly break the wicket, while there is always a chance that a ball going direct to the wicket-keeper's hand will result in the wicket-keeper upsetting his beer in the course of catching the ball. The incentive of the beer behind the stumps has been the cause of many run-outs and the replacement of the mug and its contents has been a small price to pay for the capture of a valuable wicket.

If beer and tobacco on the field have a strong moral and technical effect on your side they can have an equally strong effect on the morale of the opposition. The spectacle of your side taking the field with cigarettes and beer in hand works in a subtle psychological manner, inducing a completely false sense of confidence in your opponents and also, by the impression of casualness created, dealing a shrewd blow at any attempt to take the game too seriously. Once you can get your opponents into the same unserious and casual frame of mind as yourselves you have an immediate tactical advantage: you will be playing your natural game, and your opponents will not.

UMPIRING AND INTERPRETATION OF
THE LAWS. Even if you arrive at the scene of the match
with only five players it is essential that you should always
arrive with your own umpire. A good umpire must be
above all suspicion, but having shown that he is he must
not be above exploiting his reputation in favour of your
side. In other words, he must make the most of the fact
that to err is human, at the same time disguising this failing
so carefully that his more biased judgments appear divine
in their impartiality and wisdom.

One of the first things demanded of your umpire is that
he should be helpful, especially when your side is fielding.
He should not wait for an appeal from the bowler for
l.b.w. nor from the wicket-keeper for a catch at the wicket.
He should raise his finger as soon as he sees the ball hit
the pad or hears the sound of a snick and draw the
bowler's attention to the incident with a startled whistle
or an audibly astonished 'Cor!' The bowler can then ask

'How's that?' and receive a favourable verbal confirmation. This method of umpiral guidance was practised for many years by the local umpire of a Sussex village where I used to play. Bert could never have been accused of flagrantly biased judgement; it was just that if he sensed any doubt in the bowler's or wicket-keeper's mind and they were at all hesitant in appealing he made up their minds for them. Bert not only wanted to see his village make the most of every possible chance; he was also the local cobbler and depended for a large part of his livelihood on fixing spikes into our boots properly. Business to Bert, after all, was Business, say what you like.

In contrast to Bert, of Sussex, you occasionally encounter the umpire whose honesty and impartiality of judgement are most perversely unhelpful. My friend Edgar, who travelled for many seasons as our regular umpire when he had tired of being caught at cover every time he made the off-drive he had learned at Harrow, was always scrupulously fair so long as it didn't really matter. Such an excellent umpire both on and off the field, indeed, that in order that he should not be asked to forgo his racing on Saturdays we played all our fixtures on Sundays (he also had a car). But Edgar's eccentricity we discovered – only after nearly a season of matches – was an extreme choosiness as to *who* made the appeal. It was no good raising a communally deafening shout of 'How's that?' for a catch at the wicket *if the bowler himself didn't appeal*.

Playing once against the village where the racing stables are (it was Edgar who originally arranged this fixture), I was bowling downwind with Edgar standing at my end. A palpable catch was taken at the wicket; there was a roar from players and spectators alike.

Edgar, grinding his shooting stick more firmly into the ground, gave the batsman not out.

'What do you mean?' I asked, ' "Not Out"?' (Coarse Cricket being a democratic pastime the parry and thrust of debate and general discussion of matters of public interest is part of the fabric of our Way of Life).

'You didn't appeal.'

'I know. It was barely necessary. It was so obvious.'

'Why didn't you appeal?'

'I told you. Anyway, I didn't hear it.' (I am rather deaf in one ear).

'You should have appealed.'

'Did you hear it?'

'No. It's downwind.' (Edgar is rather deaf in one ear, too). 'But I saw it.'

'But the wicket-keeper heard it – and caught it.'

'I know. But that's not enough. The bowler's got to appeal.'

'All right. "How's that?" '

'Too late now. I've already said "not out".'

'Oh. But he *was* out, wasn't he?'

'Yes, of course. Everybody knows that.'

The meeting then passed on to other business.

Standing, or rather sitting, on his shooting-stick, at square-leg, Edgar was just as methodical in his umpiring as he was at the bowler's end. But in this position, perhaps, his interpretation of the Laws, if not so personal, gave greater satisfaction to us when we were in the field. Edgar went on the theory that *if* he made a slight error of judgement in our favour it was almost impossible to prove it. Thus a doubtful appeal for stumping would always be allowed, provided the bails were whipped off tidily and the appeal convincing, on the grounds that the batsman had lifted his heel off the ground for a fleeting and no longer re-capturable second. Similarly, in the excitement that accompanies an attempted running-out, Edgar could always justify his decision in our favour by pointing out that the batsman had neglected to ground his bat as he ran to the crease. The evidence of the photo-finish has not yet been accepted in Coarse Cricket, and if you ask me it is just as well. There is no need for it, anyway, so long as everybody understands that the Umpire's Decision is Final.

The principle guiding that final decision is one that covers all eventualities: 'If, in the opinion of the Umpire . . .' Thus we have no haggling over the M.C.C.'s latest l.b.w. rule; we have no time for calculating any Euclidean proposition concerning the ball pitching in a line described etc. If, in the opinion of the Umpire, the ball would have hit the wicket then the batsman is out and that is all there is to it. This, of course, applies only to *your* bowlers. When your side is batting, the M.C.C. rule is applied literally and your umpire's reason for giving the batsman not out is far too complicated and abstruse to explain without a set square and a book of log tables, so that – once more – the Umpire's Decision must be accepted as Final. And if this axiom is questioned then doubts are raised at once and the batsman is, of course, to be given the benefit of them.

Circumstances are held to alter cases, and the Coarse Cricket umpire who does not recognize that this applies more to your side than to your opponents is best left behind. Even if he has got a car.

SCORING. Travelling your own scorer to a Coarse Cricket match may appear, on the surface, to be just so much ostentation. The opposition, you reflect, are bound to have their own scorer, and as far as your own score book and records are concerned the whole sad story can be copied in after the match.

But to have your own scorer, experience tells you, is no more of a luxury than having your own umpire, and it is always worth while trying to find a seat in a car for him. As a race, scorers seem to come from the ranks of those whom the Organizer, in his final desperate moments, has tried to rope in to play for his side. They will have declined but added gaily: 'I'll come and score for you, if you like . . .' In the general last-minute chaos of organizing, the Organizer may be tempted to mutter a sulky thank-you and pass on to more pressing business. But he is an unwise Organizer who dismisses the offer altogether, for scorers have a knack of having a friend who has a car and wishes for nothing better than a day in the country watching Coarse Cricket. And that extra, unexpected car will prove to be very useful when the question of Transport raises its ugly head on Sunday morning.

To have one's own scorer is therefore something *en supplément* well worth aiming at though never, of course, at the expense of a playing passenger in any car. The presence of a travelling scorer can be of great moral and tactical value. The fact that you have a scorer in addition to your own umpire impresses the opposition that, in spite of your arriving seven men short, your side is well organized and that your general carefree appearance and casualness mask a basic natural competence born of good cricket breeding and expert experience.

If your scorer knows all your players by name as well as socially his presence at the scorers' table can save much embarrassment when you are in the field. It obviates, for instance, having to answer the tiresome queries bawled out

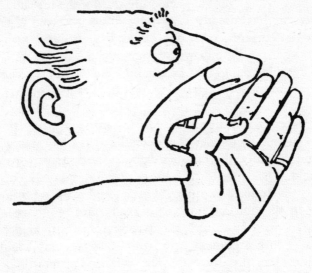

over the countryside when there is only one (opposition) scorer at work: 'Bowler's name!' – 'Who caught that?' Such questions invariably produce answers like 'Maudley-Winnington-Pauncefoot' and 'Szymanowski' and considerable delay follows as the names have to be spelt out at slow dictation speed. If such questions are not asked then the score-book is filled with rather irreverently descriptive nicknames such as are used by cloakroom attendants who check your hat and coat at smart hotels and instead of giving you a ticket mark your clothing with a label on which is written some handy mnemonic like 'Old Baldy', 'Schnozzle', or 'Flash Harry'. In Coarse Cricket an unprimed scorer will think up even less complimentary *noms de jeu* such as 'Fatty', 'Tishy', 'Shirty', 'Bandy', 'Weedy', 'Flatfoot', 'Tatcho', 'Tired Tim' or 'Dopey'.

A personal scorer can be of considerable assistance in keeping things running smoothly during the first innings when, as has already been fully discussed, your side is fielding. He is of greater importance to your side, however, in the second innings when your side is batting, for it is during this innings that he can introduce various conventions and revive certain legitimate rules to your great advantage.

There is the question, for instance, of that time-honoured schoolboy custom of crediting the batsman with a run provided the batsmen have crossed before a catch is held. This is well worth introducing and any objection that it is impossible to record a run and a wicket off one ball in the bowling analysis is easily met by giving the bowler his wicket and the batsman his run and dismissing any argument as an unnecessary complication. Besides, you say, since the non-striking batsman is now at the other end and the striking batsman was caught, not run out, there must have been a run, mustn't there?

At this point, the opposition scorer having given way to your representative's unassailable logic says very well but in that case the same rule must apply in retrospect to *his* batsman. Your scorer will register considerable astonishment at this: 'Do you mean to say you don't put down a run if the batsmen cross? But it's always done, old boy. Better put it right at once.'

The two scorers will then get together and rectify things.

Opposition Scorer: 'That makes another run for Summerfield.'

Your Scorer: 'I think you're wrong there, old boy. Summerfield was caught Maudley-Winnington-Pauncefoot, and old Pauncers always fields in the slips – fallen arches, and a nasty operation, you know. Couldn't possibly have crossed for that catch."

O.S.: 'Oh. Well, Woolford – that's another run.'

Y.S.: 'Caught Farthingale? He's the wicket-keeper. But your chap Snelling – he was caught in the deep all right. We'll give him a run.' (This generous gesture makes further successful bargaining much easier, and if Your Scorer plays his cards correctly he will more than make up on the swings what he loses on the roundabouts.)

It will be noted that in drawing attention to the affair of the batsmen crossing, your personal scorer has carefully refrained from referring to the matter until it is clearly going to be to your side's advantage to do so. If your batsmen are being skittled out by a demon bowler who sends the stumps flying in all directions then it is obviously unwise to mention anything about a run-for-a-catch; and even if one of your batsmen does qualify for this extra bonus, the scorer must quickly glance at the first innings score and judge whether few enough of the opposing batsmen were caught out to make the introduction of the convention a profitable one from your point of view. In other words, he must not play out his trump cards too soon.

The rule governing a Lost Ball, for instance, must never be invoked while your side is fielding; indeed, the fact that such a Law exists at all must not be mentioned until the time is appropriate and that is certainly not while the opposition is batting. To refer to the fact that six runs may be awarded for a lost ball during your opponents' innings is to load the dice too heavily in their favour; they will be hitting far too many straightforward sixes as it is, without giving them a bonus to which they may not even know they are entitled. If the dice are to be loaded in anyone's favour they must, of course, be loaded in yours. In the event of one of your batsmen hitting a ball in such a way that it is not immediately retrieved but another is produced with which to continue the game, your scorer will make a mental note of the fact and if, after perhaps ten minutes or so, there is still no sign of the original ball being found by the army of small boys and girls searching for it in the long grass, the nettles or the field the other side of the railway embankment, will then draw attention to the incident claiming six runs as laid down in the Laws of Cricket.

It is extremely likely that the opposition scorer will dispute the validity of your scorer's claim. Any such objection can immediately be dealt with by simple reference to the Laws of Cricket. If no copy of such Laws is available then it is up to your scorer to use personal persuasion, using a patient, patronizing tone of voice and saying, for example: 'Didn't you know about the Lost Ball rule? I thought everybody knew that one; one of the oldest Laws in cricket . . . Oh, but I assure you it *is* used in First Class Cricket . . . I remember Bill Hitch at the Oval hitting a ball out of the ground on to a tram . . . I know there aren't any trams now, I'm talking about forty years ago . . . Of course, the ball wasn't *actually* lost. They might have pinched the conductor for stealing by finding, but as far as the match was concerned it was a lost ball . . .'

The scorer can then discuss how the six runs are to be

recorded in the score-book. Six runs for the batsman, obviously, and six runs against the bowler if the hit was originally a six. And the six extra for a lost ball? He can afford to be magnanimous and put them down among the extras, thereby sparing the opposition bowler the indignity of having twelve runs scored off his one ball.

If the opposition scorer can be talked into recognizing the Law of the Lost Ball it is more than possible that he will demand retrospective recognition of the Law for his own side. As in the case of retrospective claims for batsmen crossing in mid-catch, your scorer must temper his argument against them with occasional generous gestures. He should not have much difficulty in ensuring that the whole matter reacts in his side's advantage; not only are these retrospective claims extremely difficult to prove, but he can counter all assertions that a ball was lost each time a six was hit off the Captain's bowling by pointing out that the Captain bowls *only* with a new ball and that if the Captain went on bowling after the alleged incident the ball could not possibly have been lost. Q.E.D. Since, in my experience, it is usually only the Captain who is ever hit for six, the question of other claims rarely arises.

The advantages of travelling with your own scorer, then, may be seen to be considerable when it comes to making the most of details and conventions which might otherwise be ignored. But even in the event of no batsman being caught and no balls being lost, the Coarse Cricket scorer is still worth his place in the Captain's caravan for his value as vigilator and preventive officer. For the travelling scorer is alone in being able to keep a strict watch on the tough little girl with pigtails who invariably keeps the score for the opposition in a frighteningly meticulous and efficient manner and who, if she is not very carefully watched, is nevertheless capable of slipping in an extra bye or leg-bye from time to time in order to augment the opposition's total. One of the most successful ways of countering this practice, without actually accusing the little horror of cheating, is from time to time to shout to the umpire that it is over when in fact only four or five balls have been bowled.

The pigtailed menace will immediately remonstrate. Your scorer, having carefully recorded a complete over in the bowling analysis, will show her blandly that she is quite wrong; she must have forgotten to take that phoney leg-bye into account. The umpire, of course, will meanwhile be bawling *his* point of view, protesting that the number of beans he has changed from one pocket of his coat to the other make only five with full support of the Captain who is furious at being short-changed in the over he was bowling. In the general uproar and interruption which is now confusing everything the scorer can admit his mistake and it is probable that the Captain will continue to bowl his over which, owing to one thing and another, is likely to consist of eight balls. The fact that the two extra balls have led to eight unnecessary and avoidable runs being scored is beside the point; the scorer has questioned his opposite number's accuracy, made her realize that she is being watched and that she is unlikely to be able to get away with the odd extra again.

In doing so, your scorer will have fulfilled one of his most important functions: that of guardian of Fair Play.

COSTUME AND EQUIPMENT. How often has one not stood at the corner of the Tavern at Lord's on a summer's afternoon and been approached by the newly-arrived spectator asking: who's batting? A score card or mere familiarity with the appearance of the players on the field can usually answer this question; but there are many occasions on which a score card cannot be had and the new arrival, being a lover of cricket in the abstract as it were, cannot distinguish – even if he knew – whether the blue-capped players in the field are Yorkshire or Middlesex.

How much easier things would be for the casual, myopic spectator if cricket teams wore distinctive-coloured shirts as footballers do. As things are at present fancy-class players do not even necessarily wear their county caps and sweaters in the field. They may wear a Crusaders' or M.C.C. touring cap, an England or a Hawks sweater; or no cap or sweater at all. Each year as I watch the boys of Rugby School in their pale blue shirts at Lord's so I regret that their custom has not been widely adopted; it gives their team individuality and elegance and brings a hint of colour to a game which, sartorio-aesthetically speaking, can do with it. I do not ask that cricketing dress should be vulgarized by the introduction of barrow-boys' tartan shirts; just that the familiar white-against-green of the cricket field should be varied by the discreet addition of other colours.

The virtually monochrome uniform of formal cricket does not, happily, apply to Coarse Cricket. The casual passer-by beside a village green is never in two minds as to which is the Coarse Cricket team of the two sides in action. Not only can he see which is which by the standard of the

cricket being played; he can also tell at once from the
clothes being worn by the players. Monochrome uniform-
ity of dress has never been one of the more noticeable
characteristics of Coarse Cricket. The preponderance of
brown boots, grey flannel trousers, short-sleeved tennis
shirts and the occasional rugger or French fisherman's
jersey is due to several causes. The first is largely financial:
few players can afford to buy a new outfit just for the rare
occasional game. The second is purely physical: there may
be spotless flannels hanging in the wardrobe at home, but
there are just not the figures around any longer to get into
them. The third and most frequent cause is that the players
not having played cricket since they were at prep school,
have never possessed any white flannels in their adult lifetime to grow out of and certainly do not intend to invest in
a cricketing wardrobe at their time of life.

In any case, so far from the average Coarse Cricketer's dress being anything to be ashamed of, its very individuality and unconventional form is something which a wide-awake Captain can exploit with success. A fielder in a khaki shirt, grey flannels and brown boots may be considered to possess valuable protective colouring and should be set to field on the boundary, preferably under a tree and close to the spectators, where he will be unnoticed by the batsman and from his position as invisible deep long-extra-cover can engineer (as has already been hinted) many a welcome and unexpected run-out.

Caps, sweaters and blazers are also of great psychological importance. None of these, of course, need have any association with cricket; all that is needed is some device on the garment indicating that the wearer has at some time been proficient at games – whether rugby, soccer, hockey, golf, lacrosse, billiards, squash rackets or lawn tennis is immaterial. I have even known the blazer awarded for a Half-Blue for chess to have been regarded with respect by an opposition which mistook the letters C.U.C.C. beneath the embroidered chess board to mean Cambridge University Cricket Club and to have been greatly impressed in consequence.

The wearing of colours and embroidered symbols connected with 'foreign' sports is also very helpful in explaining away any lack of skill at cricket shown by their wearers, and there is a certain snob satisfaction in being able to explain some unfortunate fielding by deep long-mid-on with the off-hand observations: 'That's Arthur Rees, you know – one of the best back-row forwards Wales ever had . . .'

The matter of caps, perhaps, is a little more difficult for

only those who have ever played cricket possess them as a
rule; there is not, so far as I know, a distinctive cap made
to be worn while playing chess or inter-university billiards.
If, however, the Organizer is willing to risk the inevitable
financial loss involved he can arrange with a sports out-
fitter to make a special cap for his players – the financial
loss, of course, will be the result of failure to get members
to pay up when they've got the caps. For the sake of cheap-
ness it is best to choose a cap in which the colours are
quartered, or (gayer still) divided into eight. This will
obviate any need for expensive embroidery of initials or
arms and when faded may be mistaken for an Oxford
Harlequins cap.

The Organizer may find a certain prejudice amongst
sports outfitters against the provision of such caps, but
with a little patience and reasoning it can be overcome.
Why any such prejudice should exist I do not know, but I
encountered it before the war when we went into Jack
Hobbs' shop in Fleet Street to order some caps for the
Coarse Cricket team then run by the editorial staff of the
Daily Express (editorial staffs always play Coarse Cricket;
the printers never – they are much too good). We pointed
to a cap in the window; it was divided into eight different
colours, and we said we wanted a dozen like that.

'That's only a sample cap, sir,' they said.

We said we knew. We didn't want that particular one;
we wanted a dozen like it.

'But it's only to show the available range of colours,'
persisted the salesman.

We said we knew that too. We wanted a dozen caps
each divided into the available colours.

In the end the salesman presumed we were barmy and

agreed reluctantly to provide us with twelve polychrome caps which never failed to cause a sensation on the field of play. When I left the *Express* and went back to the *Daily Herald* I took my cap with me and could be observed wearing it in our almost weekly match against the *Express*, thus bewildering the casual spectator more than ever who, seeing the same cap being worn on both sides, still couldn't make out which side was which.

The only article of clothing concerning which individual choice and preference should be discouraged is the tie. While to the Coarse Cricketer of experience the arrival of his fellows wearing an assortment of Hawks, Crusader, Vincent's, Authentics, England, County, Club or good-class Old School ties may give him a cosy feeling of being in company of considerable Tone, the accumulative effect on the average opposition will be virtually nil. The average opposition does not even recognize the garish and vulgarly un-English, red-and-yellow M.C.C. tie as being anything more than something to keep the trousers up with. But a team arriving with its own specially designed and exclusive tie is a team with an immediate and awe-inspiring Tone of its own. In every sense it is a team that will be regarded as without parallel, and a psychological blow of this kind struck early on in the day can have a subtle, advantageous moral effect.

As in the case of the special cap, the provision of a peculiar tie is not an expensive matter – except to the Organizer, who, as before, will find it almost impossible to recover the initial outlay involved. A hand-embroidered tie of simple design can be retailed at as little as a guinea per piece per person if a minimum of four dozen ties is ordered. This means that at the end of the first season of the introduction of the tie the Organizer will find himself with about thirty-five unsold ties on his hands and a balance of at least eight or nine guineas owing to him for those he has sold. Still, next year's always another season and there will be new players in the side who may or may not prove to be likely customers.

The design chosen for the tie is, of course, entirely a matter of the Organizer's personal taste. Simple symbolism that tells a story is usually the most effective. For my own team I devised a green tie (representing the field of play) on which were embroidered in white (a purely idealized symbol of the players in flannels) the Roman numerals VII and XIII.

It is a striking tie and never fails to inspire curiosity in those seeing it for the first time. In reply to the unvarying question: what's that tie you're wearing? all who wear it answer simply: 'It's our cricket XI.'

There will be a moment of thoughtful silence, and then: 'I see. But what do all those 8s and 15s mean?'

Ignoring the questioner's lack of education we explain that they are 7s and 13s 'because we have never yet arrived with eleven players – always either seven or thirteen.'

By way of a change the answer may sometimes be varied with the casual reply that it is, of course, the VIIth/XIIIth Hussars. This reply has not yet failed to satisfy and impress, and is very useful at cocktail parties.

The matter of Coarse Cricket equipment, like that of Coarse Cricket costume, can be left happily to the discretion of individual players. Bats, pads, batting and wicket-keeping gloves belonging to members of *your* side who are grand enough to possess them traditionally become common property for the duration of the match, and any member who is reluctant to lend his private and precious bat can quickly be over-ruled by the assurance that the bat will come to no harm as the borrower has never been known to touch the ball with a bat in his life: it is just that it is customary to carry a bat out to the wicket. A mere formality; no more.

In the likely event of none of your team arriving with any equipment of any kind (except an essential and highly personal protective device known as a 'box', which can be carried in the jacket pocket), the necessary paraphernalia can always be borrowed from the opposition dressing-room. Your two opening batsmen may have to be unusually persuasive in the matter of borrowing a couple of bats, but the batsmen who follow them in the batting order need encounter no trouble; the opposition will be out on the field of play. It is just possible that the opposition's dressing-room is locked while they are fielding, but that must be guarded against before the start of the innings. The sort of fixture, however, where a dressing-room has to be locked is not to be encouraged, for it is foreign to the spirit of Coarse Cricket.

The Captain who is wise and experienced will always carry a new ball with him to every match. This is to ensure that, on winning the toss and fielding first, he has a new ball to bowl with if the opposition cannot supply one. If by some awful mischance the Captain loses the toss and is put in to bat he should keep back the new ball until the second innings when he will make a spectacular discovery of its existence and promise it to the opposition as a present, an offer which is always gratefully accepted.

The provision by the Captain of a new ball is a little expensive if it occurs too often, but in any case a cheap ball is more useful than an expensive one; it will be knocked out of shape sooner and prove capable of many unpredictable tricks which will cause discomfort to the opposition batsmen. At the end of the innings, in order to avoid having to bat against what looks like a doll's rugger ball, the Captain should give it to the umpire pointing out its sad condition and suggesting that another – but one prays not new – ball be used for the rest of the match.

EDIBLE FUNGI. It is one of the most ancient unwritten laws of Coarse Cricket that while it is at all times permissible for deep third man and other outlying fielders to pick such mushrooms and other edible fungi as they may find on the field of play, at least 25 per cent of the amount gathered by the said fielders shall be offered to the Captain. This traditional *droit de seigneur* is no idle survival of feudalism. It is based on the principle of Fair Play. The Captain, who, when he is not bowling, is too shrewd and experienced to field anywhere but on the closely mown 'square', is denied the opportunity of picking the mushrooms himself and it is therefore only simple courtesy to offer him a share of the harvest which his position and occupation preclude him from enjoying.

EXCUSES AND EXPLANATIONS

THE BATSMAN

On being bowled playing back to a half-volley: 'An absolute snorter – a yorker like that'd have bowled Bradman . . .'

On being bowled by a full toss: 'It swung a mile, old boy – straight out of the sun . . .'

On being given out l.b.w.: 'Wasn't within miles of it! I always take a leg guard . . .'

On being caught at the wicket: 'Wasn't within miles of it! I played far too late at it . . .'

On being caught and bowled: 'It should have gone over the railway, but that damned brat falling out of its pram put me off, and I played far too soon at it . . .'

On being run out: 'Silly fool! I knew there wasn't a second one there . . .'

On being bowled first ball: 'Sorry chaps! All my fault. It's dead easy really . . .'

On being bowled first ball: 'The wicket's terrible – suicide to stay out there . . .'

On just being out, purely and simply: 'Can't see a thing – really must have a net . . .'

THE BOWLER

On being hit out of the ground: 'Sorry! If he'd played the stroke properly it would have gone straight down cover's throat . . .'

On failing to take a wicket all day: 'But what can you do if they pull your outswinger round to square-leg every time . . .'

Protest on being taken off: 'I know I'd have got him in one more over . . .'

On bowling at all: 'Haven't touched the ball since last season – shockingly out of practice . . .'

On looking at his analysis: 'I'm not surprised. The ball wouldn't turn an inch on that wicket . . .'

THE FIELDER

On dropping a catch: 'It was spinning like mad . . .'

On failing to move a yard to reach an absolute sitter: 'I thought you shouted to the other John, not me . . .'

On letting a four go through the legs: 'It was curving away like mad . . .'

THE WICKET-KEEPER

On failing to stump, run out, catch the ball or prevent a bye: 'Sorry, old man – I was unsighted . . .'

THE CAPTAIN

On congratulating the opposition on their victory and giving the world a clear glimpse of the obvious: 'I'm afraid we were a little below strength this week . . .'

GETTING HOME. The purpose of drawing stumps at 6.55 p.m. on any Sunday match has already been hinted at in an earlier section. It was not pointed out, however, that to make absolutely certain there is no further play after this, those batsmen on your side who have had their innings should be encouraged to change into civilian dress as soon as they return to the pavilion. In most cases they will need no prompting in this, for even if the match be finished with an hour or more to spare, no true Coarse Cricketer either expects or is prepared for a serious second innings after the result of the match has been decided.

To pass the time, on the other hand, there are several variants of what is known as The Beer Match to be played although, in passing, it is sad to note that in recent years there has been an increasing tendency to forget that it *is* meant to be a Beer Match and that the losers are expected to stand pints all round to the victors. Nevertheless, it must be admitted that the playing of the match can be almost as worthwhile as the prize for which it is played.

One popular form of the Beer Match is to have each side bat for thirty minutes. This speeds up the rate of play beyond all recognition and we have the welcome spectacle of the incoming batsmen running towards the wicket to save time. The variant which I personally prefer, however, is that in which everybody on the side, including the player who deposes the regular wicket-keeper, bowls one over each. This not only reveals some unexpected bowling talent, but frequently also the effectiveness of lobs, sneakers and balls bowled by the wicket-keeper which, if they ever pitched on the ground, would be devastating leg-breaks. Or so he says.

At 6.55 p.m. it would appear that the Organizer-Captain's day's work is done, for there remains for him only to collect the empty beer jugs and glasses together to return to the pub, recover his score book, return all borrowed equipment to the opposition's dressing-room and round up the odd shoes, cricket boots and socks his own side have left behind in their rush to leave the ground. On reaching the pub himself, however, the Captain becomes a full-time Organizer again for the rest of the evening. He will find that half the people who owe him money for tea have slunk away early, while those who remain complicate things almost unendurably by never having any change or, indeed, any visible means of support apart from a ready supply of promissory notes.

With the landlord's bill for food and drink and glasses broken in the dressing-room finally (thanks to your remembering to bring your cheque book) paid off, the Organizer – if he is lucky – may be able to settle down to a period of carefree social intercourse and post mortem discussion of the day's events. But it will not be for long, for as the evening draws on and closing time looms only an hour ahead there will be a general proposal that all should repair to that pub along the road everybody stopped at on the way down. Whether the proposal is accepted or not, in any case the whole question of Transport rears its ugly head once more. Passengers who came down in one car in the morning are now without transport because that particular driver has had to leave early. But after many assertions that you'll take Michael if somebody else will squeeze in David, Tony and that Old Harrovian whose name you still haven't discovered, you will find that, in the end, it is easier to get your players *from* the fixture than it was to get them to it twelve hours previously.

After closing time, on the final stage of the journey back to town, the Organizer may hope to relax. He has got his team to the ground, on and off the field, and finally launched them on their way home. It will have cost him a pretty packet but he will reflect that it was worth it; and if David, who is now in the same car with him, is complaining that he has left his shoes in The Greyhound at Chalfont St. Peter and will have to make his way through London in his socks, then at least it is no longer the Organizer's responsibility. In any case, David can pick up his shoes on the way to Great Missenden next year.

In his capacity as Captain the Organizer may reflect too that he has executed his duties satisfactorily, nursed his team to victory or an honourable defeat and afterwards exercised tact and diplomacy in making small-talk with the players' wives who showed an understandable but regrettable inclination to want to go home far too early. The Coarse Cricket Captain's work, like a woman's, is never done, and when – long after midnight – he finally gets to sleep, he does so with the full knowledge that in addition to the whole business starting up all over again the next morning he will be so stiff from bowling too long that he can hardly move to the telephone to start collecting his team for the next fixture a fortnight hence.

Perhaps there are easier ways of playing cricket; I do not know. But there are few pastimes at once so rewarding, so entertaining and stimulating for all the attendant anxieties, disappointments and expense as a good game of Coarse Cricket.

5. Last Over

HOW TO SURVIVE THE WINTER. As if the Organizer of a Coarse Cricket team had not had enough organizing to do in the summer he is often unwise enough to conceive the idea of having a Cricket Dinner during the winter. The organization of this function is very closely related to that of raising a team to play in a match. Although the Organizer is spared the problems of Trans-

port and Team-Building he is still very much faced with
the difficulties of getting a certain number of people to the
same place at the same time. The only difference between
Getting a Team Together and Getting the Team to the
Dinner is one of financial risk. If all those who have played
for the side during the season should turn up at once to
dine the Organizer had better borrow Guildhall for the
evening. But experience will teach him that it is not numbers but lack of numbers that is going to give him a head-
ache; that if he gaily tells the landlord of the pub which
is to cater for him that about twenty-five people may be
expected at 25s a head (beer, wines and spirits inclusive),
it is extremely unlikely that more than eight or nine
will turn up on the night.

The last-minute reasons given for non-attendance at the
Dinner differ very little from those offered during the
summer for being unable to play in a match; time, distance, work and family affairs are all factors which play
their part in involving the Organizer in heavy financial sub-
sidy to cover the absentees' share of food and drink laid on
for twenty-five diners and consumed by less than a third of
that number who cannot reasonably be asked to con-
tribute any more towards the total cost as originally
advertised.

After several delightful but immensely costly experiences
in organizing a Cricket Dinner personal discretion has led
me through the years to hold an Annual General Meeting
instead. In the same pub, of course, in which the dinner
was previously held, but downstairs in the saloon bar where
there is a snack bar and members can feed themselves as
they please at their own expense. As there is never by any
chance any Agenda to be considered Any Other Business

can be dealt with between the hours of 5.30–11 p.m. which happen to be the opening hours favoured by The Beehive.

How a Cricket Dinner is conducted is, of course, entirely a matter for the individual to decide. Believing that speeches tend to interrupt conversation we have always, with our team, avoided anything of the kind, preferring instead to be content with the reading out and later distribution of a duplicated Annual Report, which contains a statement of hopes, fears, prospects, fixtures, statistics, averages, comments and that survival of school-magazine days, the Critique.

In the Critique the Captain can safely let himself go with criticism and comment on the behaviour and diligence of his players in a manner denied to him on the field of play, where whenever he opens his mouth he is invariably shouted down. Sheltering behind the cold written word set down long after the heat and excitement of the summer's cricket has faded none will answer him back, and he will find himself wielding authority and commanding respect which – he will reflect sadly – he has somehow never enjoyed when it really mattered. But philosophically he will also reflect that if it weren't for the way he was treated while playing cricket, the Dinner and the Annual General Meeting would hold no surprises for him.

I had intended, when I began this book, to include an example of a typical Annual Report and Critique, but I find that they have always run into many thousands of words, and that in any case most of the incidents and principles recorded so far are common to all Coarse Cricket Teams. Only the names, places and dates distinguish my experience from yours; we all have our Davids, Michaels and Pauls.

To all who love cricket, and to the Coarse Cricketer in particular, the winter is always long. To the Captain and Organizer, however, the season is not an idle one. There are new fixtures to be arranged, new likely players to be recruited. And there are still a lot of those Ties to be sold. Accordingly no opportunity of selling them must be lost: the Dinner and as many General Meetings as can be arranged are an admirable market place, and the wise and (by now) financially embarrassed Captain must take every advantage of it.

APOTHEOSIS. There are many who, not without justification, consider that Fancy-Class Cricket is too desperately serious to be enjoyable; and I must confess that personally I would never watch a Test Match if I had the chance of playing a game of Coarse Cricket instead.

But in all fairness it must be said that first-class players are capable of providing Coarse Cricket *in excelsis*. This is on the occasion of a benefit match, which to the public watching it is an afternoon of riotous hitting, but to those behind the scenes and on the field of play is not so vastly different in character and approach from the sort of cricket you and I play on a Sunday afternoon.

So little different is it, indeed, that when I undertook, a few years ago, to organize a side to play against Jack Young's Middlesex XI for Mr Young's benefit I had a strange feeling that this was where I came in.

The more alarming financial responsibilities were taken off my shoulders by the beneficiary who, according to custom, provided us all with luncheon, tea and gallons of drink in the dressing-room. But the problems of Getting a Team Together, Getting a Team to the Match, and Getting Home were the same as confront any Coarse Cricket Organizer together with one or two which are unfamiliar.

As Captain and Organizer of a side known as A Lord's Taverners XI, I found myself not only having to consult railway timetables (just in case) but the First Class Fixtures List for the weekend of August 16 as well. This was in order to see whether any likely players were within reasonable distance of Hayes in Middlesex on the Sunday. Nottinghamshire would be at Lord's so that side could be drawn on; and was. Other players whom I had hoped would play for me, unfortunately appeared to be playing in such inaccessible spots as Dover and Eastbourne. In my mind I wrote them off; but I had reckoned without a quality which was completely strange to me: the enthusiasm and generosity of cricketers who play six days first-class cricket a week, and to whom a long cross-country journey to pay practical tribute to a popular colleague on the seventh day is no barrier. Accordingly Messrs F. R. Brown and Tribe journeyed up from Dover, Messrs Insole and Kenny from Eastbourne, and Godfrey Evans from his home in Maidstone; and all of them with as little bother as if they were off to play in the next village.

As in normal Coarse Cricket there was a great deal of I'll-be-seeing-old-so-and-so-on-Wednesday-he's-sure-to-come. It was all familiar stuff, except that Old-so-and-so would be seen on Wednesday in the dressing-room at Lord's or Old Trafford instead of that familiar pub in Kensington. And there were familiar reasons for reluctant non-acceptance too. Joe Hardstaff was at home in Nottingham, nursing an injury; John Warr, who was to be lent to me by Middlesex, had to go back to Cambridge for the day to collect some books.

But the excuse I liked best was from Peter May. He was unable to play as he was involved in a Test Match at the time. It was an excuse that made a refreshing change from the one about having to do a broadcast or fetch the kids from the seaside.

In the end, with one or two borrowings from Middlesex, it was the old story of arriving with 13 players, having feared only 48 hours previously that there would be only seven. So the Middlesex players were returned to Jack

Young, who as a Coarse Cricket Organizer needed them by the Sunday afternoon, and I was able to lead a full XI on to the field. The match card read, for the record:

Spike Hughes (Cambridgeshire and Lord's Taverners)*

F. R. Brown (Northampton, England and Lord's Taverners)

G. Evans (Kent, England and Lord's Taverners)

R. McKelvie (Free Foresters, Lord's Taverners and Hughes' VII/XIII)†

G. Tribe (Northampton and Australia)

R. T. Simpson (Notts and England)

C. Poole (Notts and England)

D. J. Insole (Essex and England)

F. Stocks (Notts)

C. J. Kenny (Cambridge Univ. and Essex)

Ray Smith (Essex)

     *Captain   †Wicket-keeper

The afternoon's cricket, which was entertainingly Coarse and carefree, I will not describe in detail, beyond mentioning that Cyril Poole hit up 91 runs in 28 minutes and that the afternoon's total was 604 runs in just under 3 hours and 30 minutes. My side lost by 40 runs or so having, in the true tradition, elected by arrangement to field first. Batting, also according to tradition, No. 11 myself, I not only made the highest score of my long career but scored more runs in that one innings than I had totalled over the whole of the previous three seasons. I made 29.

It should be explained that when, reluctantly as usual, I had to go in to bat it was not yet six o'clock, the bar was still closed and collection boxes were being taken around the ground on behalf of the Hayes Club who had lent the ground. Strict instructions, therefore, were given by Jack Young that there must be no bowling at the wicket, no stumpings and no catches held – at least, not until a respectable interval had elapsed. Otherwise, of course, the match would be at an end and the spectators would leave the ground.

Accordingly I found myself in the position of having to chase after balls yards wide of the wicket, of being harmlessly beaten by numberless spinners which left me even farther out of my crease and being dropped on all sides. I also had my pads on the wrong legs, and my bat was too short in the handle; but I hit Denis Compton's famous 'Chinaman' for 6 and was finally caught in the deep by a negligent fielder who was not working to rule and made an unnecessarily brilliant catch. Asked later in an interview how I had managed to detect the Compton 'Chinaman' I stated that as I couldn't see far enough to be able to watch his hand for a 'wrong 'un' I had played the ball on its merits when it reached me. As I was always pleased for Denis to take wickets against all-comers except those from Sussex, I did not spread this obvious secret abroad. I mention it as one final instance of the universal truth that what may apply to other kinds of cricket does not apply to Coarse Cricket, and other kinds of cricket are the poorer for it.

As middle age approached and the ground at mid-off seemed farther away from me with each succeeding year, Jack Young's benefit match proved – so far at least –

to have been my last appearance as Captain and Organizer of Coarse Cricket. There was immense personal satisfaction in the occasion, for I had realized a boyhood ambition to lead a side of first-class players (six of them Test Match cricketers), to be pestered by schoolboy autograph hunters, to hit a 6 off a bowler of international repute. I took a perverse delight too in astonishing all those who have played with me throughout the years – by making 29 runs and not bowling a single ball. Both incidents were accidental of course, for I was just going to put myself on to bowl when Jack Young declared. But most of all I look back on that match with pleasure because it confirmed what I have always believed and what I hope I have suggested successfully in this little book: that even a Timeless Test must end, but Coarse Cricket goes on for ever.

Piltdown,
    Sussex.